Global Focus

Integrated Skills through Cultural Events

OXFORD
UNIVERSITY PRESS

Oxford University Press is a department of the University of Oxford.
It furthers the University's objective of excellence in research, scholarship, and
education by publishing worldwide. Oxford is a registered trade mark of Oxford
University Press in the UK and in certain other countries.

Published in Canada by
Oxford University Press
8 Sampson Mews, Suite 204,
Don Mills, Ontario M3C 0H5 Canada

www.oupcanada.com

Library and Archives Canada Cataloguing in Publication
Fogal, Gary G. (Gary Gildo), 1974-
Global focus : integrated skills through global events / Gary Fogal.

(Culture link)
ISBN 978-0-19-544446-9

1. English language--Textbooks for second language learners. 2. Readers--History. 3.
Readers (Adult).
I. Title. II. Series: Culture link

PE1128.F64 2011   428.6'4   C2011-901413-0

Cover images (clockwise from top left): Girlfriends © Anne Clark/iStockphoto, Soccer
players © EXPA/David Rawcliffe/NewSport/Corbis, Astronaut NASA, Hoodie with
Skyline © Matthew Browning/Veer, Soldier © MILpictures by Tom Weber/Getty, Rusty
Boat © Alain Couillaud/iStockphoto.

Printed and bound in Canada.

5 6 7 — 18 17 16

Global Focus

Integrated Skills through **Cultural Events**

Gary G. Fogal

OXFORD
UNIVERSITY PRESS

Chapter and Event	Artist and Song	Genre	Chapter Preview Skill
Chapter 1 The Cold War 1	Bob Dylan, "A Hard Rain's A-Gonna Fall"	Folk	• Discussing famous quotations
Chapter 2 Music and Sport 20	Gerry and the Pacemakers, "You'll Never Walk Alone"	Rock	• Understanding / Interpreting research studies
Chapter 3 Tragedies at Sea 39	Gordon Lightfoot, "The Wreck of the Edmund Fitzgerald"	Folk	• Discussing personal experiences
Chapter 4 Bloody Sunday 58	U2, "Sunday Bloody Sunday"	Rock	• Drawing inferences from headlines
Chapter 5 Apartheid 73	Vusi Mahlasela, "Weeping"	African Folk	• Discussing hypothetical situations

Reading	Writing	Listening	Speaking
• Previewing • Stylistic analysis	• Supporting claims with evidence • Short-answer exam questions	• Following on interview • Listening for: topic, main ideas, and conclusion	• Summarizing key points
• Summarizing key points	• Developing a thesis statement	• Note-taking skills	• Thinking on your feet
• Evaluating sources of information	• Writing a persuasive essay	• Listening for cause and effect	• (Short) Presentation skills
• Reading an exam question	• Writing for an audience	• Listening for facts (from a radio program)	• Summarizing events • Speaking clearly • Expressing opinions with critical thinking • Thinking on your feet
• Paraphrasing quotations • Summaries	• How to quote source material	• Listening for gist and details • Note-taking skills	• Defending a point of view

Chapter and Event	Artist and Song	Genre	Chapter Preview Skill
Chapter 6 Race Relations in America 92	Public Enemy, "Fear of a Black Planet"	Hip Hop	• Listening to commentary and discussing
Chapter 7 The Stolen Generation 110	Archie Roach, "Took the Children Away"	Folk-Rock	• Analyzing a timeline for information
Chapter 8 Science and Crime 130	The Tragically Hip, "Wheat Kings"	Rock	• Drawing inferences from headlines
Chapter 9 Space Exploration 149	Inspiral Carpets, "Saturn 5"	Brit Pop	• Listening to commentary and discussing
Chapter 10 Elements of War 164	Arcade Fire, "Intervention"	Indie Rock	• Discussing relevance of famous quotations

Reading	Writing	Listening	Speaking
• Making inferences	• Editing and proofreading skills	• Preparing questions while listening	• Presentation skills • Thinking on your feet
• Synthesizing material • Reading exam questions	• Unity and coherence • Developing a thesis statement	• Note-taking skills • Listening for gist and details • Listening for facts • Listening for cause and effect • Listening for: topic, main ideas, conclusion	• Informal debates
• Reading for arguments and counter-arguments	• Compare-and-contrast essay	• Following a linear argument • Following an interview	• Defending an argument • Thinking on your feet
• Evaluating sources of information • Reading for arguments and counter-arguments	• Dealing with counter-arguments • Persuasive essay	• Listening for gist and details	• Thinking on your feet • Summarizing key points
• SQ3R • Reading exam questions	• Writing an in-class essay exam • Thesis statements	• Identifying logical fallacies	• Arguing with fallacies • Defending a point of view

Foreword for Teachers

This textbook has been designed with three key goals in mind: 1) developing the academic skills of English language learners; 2) developing critical skills that are paramount in an academic setting at both the secondary and tertiary level of education; and 3) focusing on developing student meta-cognitive awareness. Keeping this third goal in mind, you may find the text heavy in explanatory notes. This is not an accident. In an effort to build on student meta-cognitive awareness, instructions often go into greater depth, explaining the purpose behind the tasks students are being asked to accomplish. This adds a level of scaffolding that builds upon a traditional task-based methodology. As instructors, we may often see scaffolding as singular or one-dimensional. Recent research, however, suggests that language learning should move beyond acquiring L2 skills and cover a broader scope. This textbook is an attempt at doing so, moving students well beyond task-based instruction and into a style of education that promotes critical thinking. As such, the scaffolding here provides meta-cognitive support, giving students background information as to why they are being asked to perform certain tasks. Accordingly, the instructions may seem lengthy at times, and perhaps excessive in detail, but that is the nature of this project as a whole—building student awareness of not just how to use English, but how the learning process in general unfolds and how best learners can situate themselves inside their own learning environment. In this manner, this textbook complements both language and cognitive development.

Building a Critical Eye

As well as building language skills, many of the exercises in this book require that you critically assess the material with which you are working. These two elements (language skills and critical-analysis skills) will form the foundation of your continuing education. Wherever you see the critical eye symbol (◎) you are being asked to move beyond just building language skills.

A critical analysis of any work is asking you to engage the text. That is, to develop an academic relationship with the material you are working on (not just to read something or listen to something passively). Such demands ask for your opinion on any subject matter, and/or your analysis of it. This analysis is important, but even more crucial is your ability to clearly explain your opinion *and* to provide evidence or support for what you believe. Note the importance of these two elements: clarity and support. You need to be able to defend your beliefs clearly and concisely, and in doing so you will often have to cite evidence to support or defend your opinion. This evidence can be found in various sources: books, articles, newspapers, lecture notes, television programs, radio programs, and even, on occasion, from your life experiences. In the world of academia, providing your opinion without support is not viewed upon very highly, and you can expect instructors to reward you with poor grades for it. Certainly, this book is designed to help you with your English language skills. In addition, however, it is designed to help you critically analyze the world around you, and to help you defend your analysis with evidence and support from outside material. This book also aims to ensure that you deliver your work in a clear, concise, and academic manner.

With this textbook as a guide, your instructors and your classmates will frequently challenge your ideas—this is great. You will be challenged to explain yourself more clearly, or to provide stronger or better support for your arguments. And you will be asked to challenge the ideas of your classmates, as well as the material with which you are working. The exercises in this book will help you develop both the academic language skills required for your future success, as well as build critical-thinking skills that will allow you to adapt to new environments that go beyond the language learning classroom.

Keep in mind, then, that whenever you see the ◎ symbol, you are being asked to learn more than just a new language skill—you are being asked to assess material critically and/or defend your ideas with support.

Furthermore, the vocabulary listed in this textbook is derived from the Academic Word List. This is a collection of 570 of the most popular words used in English, in academic settings. Undoubtedly, mastering this vocabulary will prove beneficial for your continued studies in English. For a complete list of these words and the word families they represent, consult this book's companion website at www.oupcanada.com/globalfocus.

Lastly, further information regarding the various musicians and artists you will discuss in each chapter is available at the back of the textbook. Check under "Credits" for websites about the musicians included in this book.

Take a few minutes to review the material you've just read, and answer the comprehension questions below. When you are finished check your answers with a partner.

Comprehension Questions

1. Which two skills will form the foundation of your continuing education?
2. From an academic perspective, what is even more important than your opinion?
3. What should you consult if you wish to view the complete Academic Word List?
4. a) With this book as a guide, what can you expect to happen to your ideas?
   b) What should you be doing with the ideas presented by your classmates and those in this textbook?

Discussion Questions

1. What do you think it means to "engage the text"?
2. Based on your answers to questions 4 a) and 4 b) above, how and why do you think this might benefit both you and your classmates? Furthermore, how might learning this strategy be beneficial outside your school life?

The Cold War

Have you read the Foreword for Students yet, on page x? If you haven't, you should return to it and answer the questions on page xi *before* beginning Chapter 1.

Introduction

Examine the images below. What can you infer from them about the relationship between America and the former Soviet Union (also once known as the Union of Soviet Socialist Republics, or USSR, or CCCP)? What might have caused some of the tension between these two countries?

"CCCP-USA Superman" by Roman Cieslewicz, 1968, © Estate of Roman Cieslewicz / SODRAC (2011)

Previewing the Reading

Previewing skills are essential for understanding where texts lead readers. Oftentimes previewing a reading requires extensive research or note-taking during a lecture. These skills help you build context, allowing you to better understand the content of the reading material. Previewing skills also come in the form of a discussion (as you have just done in the previous exercise). In the coming chapters, you will have a chance to practise other types of previewing skills. In this chapter, you will preview the reading by discussing a quotation related to the reading.

The following is a famous line spoken in 1946 by former British prime minister Winston Churchill: "An iron curtain has descended across the continent [Europe]." As a way of previewing, combine your earlier conversations regarding the previous images with this quotation. What do you think Churchill meant by an "iron curtain"? What might it be a metaphor for? And why might the year of this quotation be important? Discuss with a partner.

⤴ The Cold War

Academic Word List (AWL) Vocabulary

The following AWL words will appear in this chapter's reading. Before completing the exercise below, skim the reading with a focus on the words in bold print. This will help you complete the table below, and will prepare you for the reading.

military	prime	tense	virtual
principle	stress	nuclear	integrity
expand	occupy	violate	apparent
individual	strategy	ignorant	sphere
diminish	resolve	debate	seek
economy	major	conclude	eventual
dominate	topic	confer	constant
secure			

Place each of the above vocabulary words under the appropriate heading in the chart below. Use a dictionary if you need help. (Word forms for charts throughout this book are based on the *Oxford Advanced Learner's Dictionary, 8th Edition*.)

Verb	Noun	Adjective	Noun & Verb	Adjective & Noun	Adjective, Noun, & Verb	Adjective & Verb

Note that AWL words may exist in various forms. Words in the same family as *economy*, for example, are as follows: *economic, economical, economically, economics, economies, economist, economists,* and *uneconomical*. For a complete list of each word's family, consult a listing of the AWL, available online.

The Cold War at a Glance...

1   In 1945, the United States and the Soviet Union were allies, successfully defeating Adolf Hitler's Nazi Germany. Within just a few years, however, wartime allies became enemies, and the two

countries began a cold war—a war of political, **military**, **economic**, and ideological **tension** that stops just short of **military** engagement.

Cold War Background

2   How did wartime friends so quickly turn into Cold War enemies? Who started the Cold War? Was it the Soviets, who broke promises on their agreements to allow the people of Eastern Europe to determine their own political future? Or was it the Americans, who **ignored** the Soviets' legitimate **security** concerns, **sought** to intimidate the world with the atomic bomb, and pushed relentlessly to **expand** their own international influence and market **dominance**?

3   Meetings between the American president Franklin D. Roosevelt, British **prime** minister Winston Churchill, and Soviet general secretary Joseph Stalin began as early as 1943. They met in Iran to coordinate a **strategy** to defeat Hitler, and Poland, which sat in an unfortunate position between enemies Russia and Germany, became a **topic** for heated **debate**. The Poles, then under German **occupation**, had two governments-in-exile: one Communist and one anticommunist. Unsurprisingly, the leaders of these three countries disagreed over which Polish government should be allowed to take control after the war. For Stalin, the Polish question was a matter of the Soviet Union's vital **security** interests; Germany had invaded Russia through Poland twice since 1914, and more than 20 million Soviet citizens died in World War II. Stalin's concerns were in opposition to the Anglo-American values of self-determination. They believed the Poles ought to be allowed to make their own decision over whether or not to become a Soviet satellite country.

4   At the next **major conference** in 1945, the leaders of the US, UK, and USSR were able to reach a number of important agreements—settling border disputes, creating the United Nations, and organizing the postwar **occupations** of Germany and Japan. In the end, agreements reached were not so much a true compromise as a useful misunderstanding among the three leaders. Stalin left happy he had won Anglo-American acceptance of Soviet control of Eastern Europe; Roosevelt and Churchill left happy they had won Stalin's acceptance of the **principle** of self-determination. However, what would happen if Eastern European countries **sought** independence from Soviet control? Future disputes were **virtually** inevitable.

After World War II

5   After the unexpected death of the American president in 1945, Vice-President Harry S. Truman—a former Missouri senator with only a high-school education, and who had served just 82 days as vice-president—suddenly became the president of the United States. Truman viewed the Soviets' later interventions in Eastern Europe as a simple **violation** of the aforementioned agreements, proof that Stalin was a liar who could never be trusted. Truman quickly created a hard-line position, **resolving** to counter Stalin's **apparently** insatiable drive for power by blocking any further **expansion** of the Soviet **sphere** of influence. Under Truman, containment of Communism soon came to **dominate** American foreign policy. The Cold War had begun.

6   In the decades that followed, a massive **military** build-up occurred in both the United States and the Soviet Union. Both viewed their ideologies (American capitalism and Soviet Communism) as **dominant**, and both made attempts to **expand** their political, **military**, **economic**, and ideological interests. Examples of either **expanding** or protecting their ideologies include the Korean War (1950s), the Cuban Missile Crisis (1962), and the Vietnam War (1960s). A **major** symbol of the Cold War (as well as a symbol of its **conclusion**) was the Berlin Wall, built in 1961 by the East Germans as a deterrent for people trying to cross into West Germany from the Soviet-controlled East.

Paragraphs 1-5 adapted from "Causes of the Cold War" by Shmoop University, Inc. (www.shmoop.com)

7   Although historians disagree over the exact date and events that led to the end of the Cold War, most agree that **stress** levels began to **diminish** in 1985, and that the Cold War drew to a close in 1991. One of the most poignant symbols of its end was the fall of the Berlin Wall in 1989.

The Cuban Missile Crisis

8   The Cold War–era was filled with intense levels of **stress** and anxiety. The world was often on full alert, fearing an **eventual nuclear** war between the two superpowers that would wipe out humanity. The Cuban Missile Crisis marked one such nuclear threat. In 1962, the Soviet general secretary Nikita Khrushchev signed a deal with Cuba allowing the USSR to place nuclear missiles on Cuban soil (a Communist-controlled island situated 150 kilometres from the United States). The Americans considered this a **major** threat to their safety, as these missiles could easily reach anywhere in the States within minutes. For weeks, US president John F. Kennedy and the Soviet leader exchanged messages and threats. During this time both militaries prepared for a nuclear war and people around the world experienced extremely high stress levels—many believed a nuclear war was inevitable. This particular crisis lasted more than a month before a deal was reached in November 1962 to end the crisis.

Cuba's location in the Caribbean

Coping with the **Stress**

9   With **constant** fear imbuing their daily lives, angst and a general feeling of powerlessness and torment filled the psyche of many **individuals**. Out of these emotions grew a peace movement overflowing with protests marches and calls for disarmament. Artists and musicians around the world began to question the **integrity** of the Cold War. In 1962, Bob Dylan wrote "A Hard Rain's A-Gonna Fall," a product of the **stress** and anxiety people felt at this time in history.

Fill in the table below with three words from this article that are *not* from the AWL, but that are new for you.

Word	Part of Speech	Definition	Sample Sentence

Share your table with a partner.

Reading for Details

The following statements are incorrect. Correct them on the lines below.

1. The first meeting between the three allies was in 1945, after the defeat of Nazi Germany.

   _____

2. Germany was a security threat for the Soviets because it was between the USSR and Poland.

   _____

3. Germany was worried Poland would once again be invaded by the Soviet Union.

   _____

4. Truman was interested in promoting the expansion of the Soviet sphere of influence.

   _____

5. Historians agree that stress levels began to increase in 1985.

   _____

Share your answers with a partner. Try to use this chapter's AWL vocabulary as often as you can in your discussion.

 Discussion Questions

Discuss the following questions with a partner.

1. In paragraph 1, the writer defines a cold war as a war of political, military, economic, and ideological tension that stops just short of military engagement. Why do you think this is called a "cold" war? Can you think of another adjective that might be just as appropriate?

2. At the end of paragraph 4, the writer asks a *rhetorical question*. First, rewrite the question in your own words and make sure you clearly understand it. Second, try to answer it with your partner, and provide reasons to support your view.

   _____

3. Paragraph 6 discusses the ideologies of American capitalism and Soviet Communism. What are some distinguishing features of these two ideologies?

4. Look for more rhetorical questions in the reading. What does each of these questions force the reader to do? Do they influence the reader at all? Discuss in detail with your partner.

> *rhetorical question*—a question that does not require an answer, but is asked in order to produce a persuasive effect or to make a statement
>
> Example: *Guns are dangerous weapons. Does anyone enjoy being shot at? Gun control is a serious problem.*
>
> The assumption is that no one would enjoy being shot at. The question is used here as a persuasive rhetorical device in an argument supporting gun control.

Vocabulary Practice

Definitions

Match the words below with their appropriate definitions.

1. prime 2. virtual 3. principle 4. apparent 5. diminish 6. seek 7. eventual	_____ to look for something or somebody; to try to obtain or achieve something
	_____ easy to see or understand; that which seems to be real or true, but may not be
	_____ almost or very nearly the thing described, so that any slight difference is unimportant; made to appear to exist by the use of computer software
	_____ main; most important; of the best quality; the time in your life when you are strongest or most successful; to prepare somebody for a situation so that they know what to do, especially by giving them special information
	_____ to become or to make something become smaller, weaker, etc.; to make somebody or something seem less important than they really are
	_____ a moral rule or a strong belief that influences your actions; a law, a rule, or a theory on which something is based; a general or scientific law that explains how something works or why something happens
	_____ happening at the end of a period of time or of a process

Definitions taken or adapted from *Oxford Advanced Learner's Dictionary 8th Edition* by A. S. Hornby © Oxford University Press 2010. Reproduced by permission.

The word *prime* can be a noun, adjective, or verb. In the above definition, underline the definition of the noun, circle the definition of the adjective, and put square brackets [ ] around the verb. Then, write a sentence below that matches each of these definitions of *prime*.

1. _____

2. _____

3. _____

The word *tense* can also be a noun, adjective, or verb. Write a definition for each function of *tense*, and provide a sample sentence for each. Use a dictionary if you need help.

1. Definition: _____

   Sentence: _____

2. Definition: _____

   Sentence: _____

3. Definition: _____

   Sentence: _____

Expanding Lexical Concepts

Collocations

What is a collocation? The *Oxford Advanced Learner's Dictionary* defines a collocation as two or more words often being used together, in a way that happens more frequently than would happen by chance.

For example: *light rain* or *completely forgot*

In English, collocations are words that are frequently used together. Collocations are important to know because English contains thousands of them. Use the AWL vocabulary in the text box to form high-frequency collocations with the words below.

tense	stress	expand
individual	resolve	debate
economy	topic	

1. booming, dynamic, healthy, sound, stable, strong, fragile, stagnant, weak, recovering
    _____

2. feel, look, seem, sound, incredibly, increasingly, a bit, a little, rather _____

3. broad, narrow, main, complex, difficult, essay, lecture, controversial, sensitive, consider / discuss / focus on / write on a/the _____

4. fully, successfully, adequately, peacefully, easily, rapidly, eventually, finally, attempt / take steps / try / be unable / fail to _____

5. heated, intense, lively, lengthy, public, political, have / hold / contribute to a, under
    _____

6. significantly, further, rapidly, gradually, suddenly, steadily, eager / hope / plan to
    _____

7. considerable, severe, unnecessary, emotional, mental, physical, psychological, economic, financial, show signs of, avoid, alleviate, ease, relieve _____

8. outstanding, talented, powerful, creative, unique, like-minded, qualified _____

Using Collocations

Fill in the blanks using the AWL word in parentheses with the correct collocation from the list above. More than one answer may be suitable at times.

1. Final exams create an _____ atmosphere around university campuses across the country. (tense)

2. Athletes experience high levels of psychological and _____ (stress)

3. Many companies are _____ in developing countries. (expand)

4. The _____ for the mid-term examination required that we write about a sensitive issue. (topic)

5. The two groups took _____ their differences. (resolve)

6. A _____ exists when excessive economic progress fails to be seen over long periods of time. (economy)

7. Employers often seek out the most _____ to fill job vacancies. (individual)

8. The political candidates in the election had a lengthy _____ in Central Park. (debate)

Word Forms

Fill in the blanks with the appropriate form of the AWL vocabulary.

1. During important sporting events many hotels reach their maximum _____ levels.
   a) occupying   b) occupancy   c) occupation   d) occupational

2. Students in _____ of curfew rules often face strict punishments.
   a) violated   b) violating   c) violation   d) violate

3. Historians often debate Napoleon's role as a military _____.
   a) strategist   b) strategists   c) strategically   d) strategic

4. _____ regarding the law is rarely an acceptable defence in the court of law.
   a) Ignorance   b) Ignoring   c) Ignores   d) Ignorant

5. Many planets, including Earth, are not a perfect _____ shape.
   a) sphere   b) spheres   c) spherical   d) spherically

6. The lawyer presented _____ evidence; as such the defendant was set free.
   a) conclusive   b) concluding   c) inconclusive   d) inconclusively

7. The United States and the former Soviet Union were the two _____ figures in the Cold War.
   a) dominance   b) dominated   c) dominate   d) dominant

8. The delegates at the _____ all had a chance to confer with each other.
   a) conference   b) conferring   c) conferred   d) confer

9. The _____ demands of her boss led her to quit her job.
   a) constancy   b) inconstancy   c) constantly   d) constant

10. Freshmen students of any age often feel high levels of _____ while they are adjusting to a new academic environment.
    a) insecure   b) insecurity   c) secure   d) securing

Before Moving On...

About Folk Music

The term *folk music* originated in the 1800s. The music was not recorded; rather, it was passed down orally from one generation to the next. A key element of folk music is that its lyrics tell a tale, often depicting real-life situations or a story involving a local community. Each country has its own folk-music tradition. Some examples of traditional instruments include the Indian sitar, the Australian didgeridoo, the Japanese shamisen, the Persian lute, and the American banjo. Having lost popularity for some time, after World War II folk enjoyed a revival of sorts, as musicians such as Bob Dylan, Joan Baez, Joni Mitchell, and Neil Young all produced music, in part, within the folk genre. Folk music itself has since altered and changed, mixing with other styles to produce, for example, folk-rock—a fusion of folk and rock and roll. As the song you are about to hear will demonstrate, Bob Dylan began his career in the folk tradition before widening his own musical talents.

A Cold-War Song: "A Hard Rain's A-Gonna Fall"

About the Artist

Born in 1941 in the American state of Minnesota, Bob Dylan (named Robert Allen Zimmerman at birth) moved to New York in 1961 to pursue a career in music. With his unique voice and gifted command of the language, within just a few years Dylan exploded on to the American music scene, soon securing himself a position as one of the most influential figures in modern music history. With his roots in American folk music, over the next decades Dylan continued to reinvent his musical style. Many of his early songs, such as "A Hard Rain's A-Gonna Fall," written when he was only 21 years old, were taken up as anthems of peace and protest. Well known as a master lyricist, Dylan is to date the only musician ever nominated for the Nobel Prize in Literature—a testament to the poetic nature of his work. In 2004, American magazine *Newsweek* called Bob Dylan "the most influential cultural figure now alive." Despite his age, Dylan still maintains a rigorous concert schedule.

Listen to the song and try to fill in the blanks. You will have two opportunities to hear it.

Bob Dylan—"A Hard Rain's A-Gonna Fall"

Oh, where have you been, my blue-eyed son?
And where have you been, my darling young one?
I've _____ on the side of twelve misty mountains
I've walked and I've _____ on six crooked highways
I've stepped in the middle of seven sad forests   5
I've been out in front of a _____ _____ _____
I've been ten thousand miles in the mouth of a graveyard
And it's a hard, it's a hard, it's a hard, it's a hard
It's a hard rain's a-gonna fall.

Oh, what did you see, my blue-eyed son?   10
And what did you see, my darling young one?
I saw a _____ _____ with wild wolves all around it
I saw a highway of diamonds with nobody on it
I saw a black branch with blood that kept drippin'
I saw a _____ _____ _____ _____ with their hammers a-bleedin'   15
I saw a white ladder all covered with water
I saw ten thousand talkers whose _____ were all broken
I saw guns and _____ _____ in the hands of young children
And it's a hard, it's a hard, it's a hard, and it's a hard
It's a hard rain's a-gonna fall.   20

Oh, what did you hear, my blue-eyed son?
And what did you hear, my darling young one?
I heard the _____ _____ _____ _____, it roared out a warnin'
I heard the roar of a wave that could drown the whole world
I heard _____ _____ _____ whose hands were a-blazin'   25
I heard ten thousand whisperin' and _____ _____
I heard one person starve, I heard many people laughin'

I heard the song of a _____ who died in the gutter*
I heard the sound of a clown who cried in the alley
And it's a hard, it's a hard, it's a hard, it's a hard   30
It's a hard rain's a-gonna fall.

Oh, what did you meet my blue-eyed son?
And what did you meet, my darling young one?
I met a _____ _____ beside a dead pony
I met a white man who walked a black dog   35
I met a young woman whose _____ _____ _____
I met a young girl, she gave me a _____
I met one man who was wounded in love
I met another man who was wounded in hatred
And it's a hard, it's a hard, it's a hard, it's a hard   40
It's a hard rain's a-gonna fall.

And what'll you do now, my blue-eyed son?
And what'll you do now my darling young one?
I'm a-goin' back out 'fore the rain starts a-fallin'
I'll walk to the depths of the _____ _____ _____   45
Where the people are many and their _____ _____ _____ _____
Where the pellets* of poison are flooding their waters
Where the home in the valley meets the damp dirty prison
And the _____ _____ is always well hidden
Where hunger is ugly, where the souls are forgotten   50
Where black is the color, where none is the number
And I'll _____ it and _____ it and _____ it and _____ it
And reflect from the mountain so all souls can see it
And I'll _____ _____ _____ _____ until I start sinkin'
But I'll know my songs well before I start singin'   55
And it's a hard, it's a hard, it's a hard, and it's a hard
It's a hard rain's a-gonna fall.

*Song Vocabulary

gutter (noun): a channel at the edge of a road where water collects and is carried away to drains
pellet (noun): a small hard ball of any substance; often of soft material that has become hard

Definitions taken or adapted from *Oxford Advanced Learner's Dictionary 8th Edition* by A. S. Hornby © Oxford University Press 2010. Reproduced by permission.

Listen Again!

Listen to the song again and double-check your answers. When you are finished, check your answers with a partner.

Song Survey

In the last column provide a reason for your choice.

1. Do you like songs that deal with serious issues?	Yes	No	
2. Would you listen to more songs by Bob Dylan?	Yes	No	
3. Would you recommend this song to your friends?	Yes	No	

4. Is this the kind of song your parents would listen to?	Yes	No	
5. Do you know any other songs about a serious topic? If yes, what is the song about?	Yes	No	

Share your answers with a partner.

Song Discussion

◉ Discuss the following questions in small groups.

1. a) There are many repetitive phrases used in this song. What effect does this create for the listener? Is it a positive technique or a negative technique? Why do you think so?
   b) Identify the rhetorical questions used in the song. Why do you think Dylan uses them so frequently? What effect does this create for the listener?
2. Bob Dylan once said, regarding the writing of this song, "Every line in it is actually the start of a whole new song. But when I wrote it, I thought I wouldn't have enough time alive to write all those songs so I put all I could into this one." Examine three or four lines of the song with a partner and discuss how each line could have started a new song. What might each new song have been about?
3. Many people argue that Bob Dylan has a terrible voice, and that it is his songwriting abilities that make him great. Based on this song, do you agree or disagree with this comment? Why, or why not?
4. Think about the reading you did earlier in this chapter. How are the topic of the reading and the lyrics of this song related? Look for evidence in the lyrics (images or word choices) to support your ideas.
5. What kind of topics do the songs you listen to talk about? How are they different from these lyrics?

🎧 Focus on Listening

Skills Focus: Following an Interview or Conversation

Being able to clearly understand questions in a discussion will allow you to participate in conversations freely and answer questions directly. This listening comprehension skill is important for everyday conversations with friends, but more importantly, during discussions with your instructors and classmates and in a job interview. Being able to listen well requires that you combine various tasks. You need to:

a) establish the context
b) establish who is speaking
c) establish the topic
d) understand the questions
e) understand the responses
f) understand any concluding comments

Note that the order of some these may change. For example, knowing the title of the piece might help you establish the topic (c) before you even begin to listen. Some of these also rely on each other, depending on the situation and the speakers. However, keep in mind that all of this information eventually needs to be processed in your brain at the same speed at which the information is being given. The following will help you with this.

Skills in Practice

Perform an Internet search for interviews with or about Bob Dylan. One excellent interview is titled "Tangled Up in School: Teaching Dylan in Boston," produced by NPR. You will find many other options for audio or video interviews if you search for "Bob Dylan interview." When you have found a suitable interview to watch or listen to, follow the instructions below.

a) Establish the context. Based on the title of the interview you found, what might you expect the interview to be about?

_____

_____

b) Establish who is speaking. Next, listen to the beginning of the interview and answer the following questions:
Who are the two speakers (what are their names and if possible, what are their jobs)?

_____

_____

Are you listening to an interview or a conversation? (establishing the context)

_____

c) Establish the topic. What kind of background information is provided at the beginning? Listen to the beginning of the interview again.

_____

_____

_____

_____

In one sentence, summarize what the topic of this piece will be.

_____

_____

d) Understand the questions. Next, listen to the entire piece and concentrate on any questions that the interviewer raises. List the questions below as best you can.

1._____
2._____
3._____
4._____
5._____
6._____
7._____

e) Understand the answers. Listen to the entire piece again, focusing on the answers to the questions you noted above. Take notes below.

1._____

2._____

3._____

_____

4._____

_____

5._____

_____

6._____

_____

7._____

_____

f) Understand any concluding comments. Listen to the interview's conclusion again. What kind of information is provided here? Make a few notes below.

_____

_____

_____

_____

Bringing It All Together

Review your answers to exercises (a) through (f) above. Listen to the piece again, and try to bring all of these elements (a–f) together. Try to understand all the information as you hear it. Listen to the interview as many times as you feel are necessary. Remember that being able to identify and understand all of these elements in a conversation or interview is essential for your future success.

Focus on Speaking

Skills Focus: Summarizing Key Points

This skill requires that you focus on the key ideas of a reading or listening piece, and that you restate these ideas in your own words. Summarizing is very different from paraphrasing or quoting (see Chapter 5). Summaries are generally much shorter than the original piece, and provide a broader overall sense of what was read or discussed, instead of going into great detail. A summary can be divided into four parts: a short introduction, the goal of the piece, the conclusion, and your opinion. The following expressions will help you with completing your summary:

I. Introduction
This (radio / TV program / reading / essay / article / story / chapter / paragraph / etc.) is about…
This _____ deals with…
This _____ is concerned with…
The purpose of this _____ is…
The subject of this _____ is…

II. The Goal of the Piece
The (speaker / writer / author / host / protagonist / etc.) is intent on showing…
The _____ wants / hopes / intends to show…
The _____ is concerned about…

The _____ mentions / points out / indicates that…
According to the _____ …

III. The Conclusion of the Piece
      The (speaker / writer / author / host / protagonist / etc.) concludes that…
      In the end…
      In the end the _____ suggests that…
      The _____ concludes by…
      The _____ comes to the conclusion that…
      After considering …, the _____ comes to the conclusion that…

 IV. Your Opinion (note the importance of giving a *reason* for your opinion)
      In my opinion / view… because….

      In this respect, I believe that… because….

      With regard to…, I think / believe that… because….

      Overall, I think / feel / believe / suspect that… because….

Skills in Practice

Exercise A

Imagine that your friend is a big fan of Bob Dylan and that she missed the interview that you selected earlier in this chapter's Listening section. Later in the evening you meet her at a coffee shop to chat. Your friend asks you if you heard the Bob Dylan interview today. You answer yes. Your friend is eager to hear about it—summarize the interview for your friend. Don't forget to include your opinion about the interview.

Exercise B

Return to the Internet to search for an interview with your favourite musician or music group. Prepare a summary of the interview, and share it with a classmate or a small group. While you are preparing keep in mind what you studied in this chapter's Listening section. When you are finished sharing your summary, rotate into another group, or change partners, and share your summary again. The more you practise, the better you will become not only at speaking English, but also at being able to identify the interview's key points and to emphasize them in your summary. Accordingly, you may make changes to your summary as you begin with a new partner or group. Also, do not forget to include your opinion about the interview.

Focus on Reading

Skills Focus: Stylistic Analysis

Understanding how writers use language as a tool to express ideas can help you understand how language works. Furthermore, this understanding will help you to become a better writer. A stylistic analysis of a text studies how authors use specific parts of speech and literary devices to create meaning. The following is a list of 15 parts of speech and literary devices. Take a few minutes to review them.

1. Abstract Nouns: nouns that are a concept, idea, experience, state of being, trait, quality, or other entity that cannot be experienced with the five senses
    (dreams, faith, culture)

    _____ *line 53: so all souls can see it >> souls*

2. Concrete Nouns: nouns that you can experience with your senses
    (car, tree, ice cream)

3. Gradable Adjectives: adjectives that can vary in intensity
    (good, better, best)

4. Non-gradable Adjectives: adjectives that are absolutes
    (dead, alive, wet, pregnant)

5. Stative Verbs: verbs that indicate unchanging or static situations
    (love, think, believe)

6. Dynamic (or Action) Verbs: verbs that indicate action
    (jump, swim, eat)

7. Adversative Conjunction: conjunctions that indicate an opposing situation
    (She was hungry, *but* she had nothing to eat.)

8. Anaphora: repeating a sequence of words at the beginning of a sentence, thereby giving the sequence emphasis
    (*I will* be strong. *I will* be healthy. *I will* do my best. *I will* survive. *I will* be me.)

9. Alliteration: the repetition of consonant sounds
    (The *s*hip *s*ailed *s*ilently on the *s*outhern *s*eas.)

10. Assonance: the repetition of similar vowel sounds
    (The fr*ee* b*ee* will *ea*t me.)

11. Synecdoche: a part of something larger that is used to refer to the whole
    (The *keel* drove forward in the water. >> *Keel* is used here to represent the entire boat.
    The trouble in *Washington* is that... >> *Washington* is used here to represent the entire US government.)

12. Hyperbole: a figure of speech that uses excessive exaggeration
    (I told you a *million times* to stop!)

13. Personification: giving human qualities to animals or objects
    (The *roses smiled* in the wind; The *pencil laughed* on the page; The *bus* was left *weeping* after the accident.)

    _____

14. Poetic Licence: linguistic freedom given to poets that allows them to alter the normal standards of grammar, syntax, or pronunciation in order produce work that more accurately reflects the image or sound they want to achieve
    (*I'm gonna* come back. She *ain't got to* be free.)

    _____

15. Add one more to the list here. (You already studied it earlier in this chapter.)

    _____

    _____

    _____

Skills in Practice

Bob Dylan uses each of these parts of speech and literary devices in the song "A Hard Rain's A-Gonna Fall." Reread the lyrics. On the line below each part of speech or literary device listed, provide an example of each device from "A Hard Rain's A-Gonna Fall." Include the line number for easy referencing. Number 1 has been done for you.

    When you are finished, discuss your answers with a partner. (Note that each of you may have found different examples.)

Focus on Writing

Skills Focus: Supporting a Claim with Evidence

With a partner, list different types of questions an instructor may ask you on an exam.

_____ *true or false question* _____   _____

_____   _____

_____   _____

Imagine that you are writing a short-answer exam, meaning the questions will require you to answer in a single paragraph (an expository paragraph) instead of an essay. Here is a sample question: *Demonstrate how Bob Dylan uses four different literary devices to support the theme of humanity's destruction of nature in the song "A Hard Rain's A-Gonna Fall."* With a partner discuss what approach or steps you would take to answer this question.

    As you develop academically, you will find that different styles work for different people. Below is a list of steps you could take to answer this question. Adapt these steps to best fit your learning style:

1. Make sure you understand the question clearly. (We will focus on this skill in Chapter 4.)
2. Identify the literary devices used in the song. (You have already done this in the previous exercise.)
3. Brainstorm.
4. Choose which four literary devices you think most clearly answer the question.
5. Develop a topic sentence.

A Quick Review

The topic sentence is the first sentence in an expository paragraph. It should always contain:

1. the topic; and
2. the controlling idea.

In its function, it resembles the thesis statement in an essay. In the following examples, the topic is bolded while the controlling idea is in blue:

Developing effective academic skills requires that you **focus on three specific areas**. (Then you would go on to discuss these areas.)

There are numerous reasons why **riding a bicycle is better for your health than jogging**. (Then you would go on to discuss these reasons.)

_____

_____

6. Begin to focus on how you will defend your claim or your argument (that literary device X supports the theme in the question).

In this chapter we are going to focus on steps 5 and 6.

Skills in Practice

First, study the examples in the A Quick Review box. In the lines provided there, write another example. Underline the topic and circle the controlling idea.

Second, develop a topic sentence for the following short-answer exam question: *Demonstrate how Bob Dylan uses four different literary devices to support the theme of humanity's destruction of nature in the song "A Hard Rain's A-Gonna Fall."*

_____

_____

_____

Third, begin to answer the question. The first paragraph has been done for you below.

Note that this question requires that you do more than just write a grammatically correct paragraph. You are being asked to critically analyze a piece of text. This requires that you move beyond language learning and that you engage academically with the text you are working with.
Study the sample below.

1. Bob Dylan uses the literary device of personification to demonstrate the theme of humanity's destruction of nature.[A] In line 5, Dylan writes "seven sad forests."[B] Here, the human quality of sadness is attached to nature—a forest.[C] This creates a sympathetic image in the listener's mind.[D] This literary device tries to involve the listener in the song by creating morose and sad feelings specifically about the destruction of a forest.[E] As a consequence, this image, created by the literary device personification, supports the idea of humanity's destruction of nature.[F]

In the example above, note the topic sentence (sentence A). Note how the writer has used evidence from the text to support his idea (sentence B), and that he has provided a reference for where it came from (line 5). Note too how this evidence is explained (sentences C, D, and E). Finally, note how the evidence (the literary device personification) is connected to the theme of the song (sentence F). This part of the exam question is quickly and efficiently answered.

◉ Using paragraph number 1 as a model, continue to answer the sample exam question.

2. _____
_____
_____
_____
_____
_____

3. _____
_____
_____
_____
_____

4. _____
_____
_____
_____
_____
_____

Additional Vocabulary

You will find this section at the end of every chapter. It is a place for you to keep track of new vocabulary words that you may have learned that are *not* included in the AWL.

Word	Part of Speech	Definition	Sample Sentence

Chapter **2**

Music and Sport

Introduction

With a partner discuss the connection between music and sports. This includes professional sports and your own exercise habits. How are the two related? When do the two mix, and why? Is this a beneficial mix? If yes, for whom? Use the photos below to help start your discussion.

Previewing the Reading

The following table compares information regarding two studies on sports medicine. Each study examined the same question: *Does pill X aid in recovery after knee surgery?* Study the table, and then discuss the questions below with a partner.

Research Factors	Research Study A	Research Study B
1. Research performed by:	Biology professor at a famous university	Team of medical doctors at a small hospital
2. Number of people examined:	81	229
3. Number of factors analyzed:	5	12
4. The people in the group were the same: a) age	No (24–36 years old)	No (16–24 years old; 30–55 years old)
b) sex	Yes (all males)	No (59% male; 41% female)
c) race	Yes (Caucasian)	No (41% Caucasian; 33% Hispanic; 20% African-American; 6% Asian)
d) body type	Yes (athletic build)	No (57% athletic build; 25% mildly overweight; 18% mildly underweight)
5. Length of the study:	16 months	8 years
6. Funding (who paid for the study to be done):	Private company	Government research funding

1. Discuss each research factor with your partner. What influence might the differences in how Research Studies A and B approached each factor have had in the results of the studies?
2. Would you consider the results of both of these studies to be acceptable? Give reasons to support your view. Would you trust the results of one study over the other? Why, or why not?

Music and Sport

Academic Word List (AWL) Vocabulary

The following AWL words will appear in this chapter's reading. Before completing the exercise below, skim the reading with a focus on the words in bold print. This will help you complete the table below, and will prepare you for the reading.

statistic	contradict	analogy	significant
physical	release	utilize	enhance
brief	appropriate	research	task
instance	classic	despite	accurate
interpret	prior	visual	scheme
regulate	benefit	draft	indicate
perceive	period	mental	relax
target	role	define	distinct
promote	induce	motive	aid

Place each of the above vocabulary words under the appropriate heading in the chart below. Use a dictionary if you need help.

Verb	Noun & Verb	Adjective & Noun	Adjective	Noun	Noun, Verb, & Adjective	Verb & Adjective	Preposition	Noun, Adverb, & Adjective

Music and Sport at a Glance...

1   Although somewhat outdated by its 1960s rock melody, "You'll Never Walk Alone" was arguably the first major pop-rock hit to be adopted by the sporting world. In 1963, soon after its **release**, fans of Liverpool—an elite team in the English Premier football league—**interpreted** the song's lyrics as **analogous** to their feelings for their favourite team. Liverpool fans began to sing this song in unison before the start of home games. This became a constant at Liverpool matches. "You'll Never Walk Alone" quickly **defined** itself as one of the first of many sports anthems to be adopted by teams and fans around the world, and in various sports.

Music and the Athlete

2   Sports anthems exist for a variety of reasons. They provide entertainment for fans while athletes warm-up, they maintain a tradition (or in the case of "You'll Never Walk Alone," give rise to a tradition), and they provide **motivation** for athletes to perform at their best. Music, it seems, is **distinct** in that it provides athletes with an extra rush of adrenalin that allows them to prepare for an athletic **task**, and, as a result of this added focus, allows them to perform better. But, is this statement actually true? Athletes seem to enjoy listening to music while they are training or preparing to compete, whether it's hip hop or hard rock broadcast over a loudspeaker, or calmer music listened to with earphones. Many athletes believe that music **aids relaxation** or helps them get into a rhythm necessary for a smooth workout. There is also the belief that uptempo music can actually help individuals move faster during a training session, leading to a higher-quality workout.

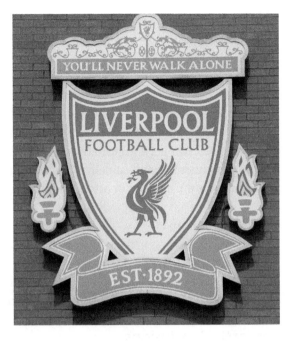

Music, Sport, and Science

3   But is music really that **beneficial**? To determine the actual effects of upbeat music on performance, scientists at Southern Connecticut State University recruited 12 female collegiate basketball players to run on a treadmill to the point of near exhaustion. Their heart rates were **regulated**, and they performed at about 85 to 90 percent capacity on three different occasions. In the first **instance**, the athletes listened to popular, upbeat rock music while running; in the second, they listened to ambient sounds from a nearby basketball game; and in the third, they listened to nothing. The upbeat music was expected to motivate the athletes and make it easier for them to deal with the stress of running. However, **perceived** exertion and heart rate were the same in all three cases, **indicating** that the music did not make the exertions feel easier or lead to lower cardiovascular stress. Nevertheless, the athletes were able to stay on the treadmills about four minutes longer while listening to upbeat music, compared to listening to a game or to nothing at all. This effect was not **statistically significant**, although it may have been if a larger sample of athletes had been used.

4   Although upbeat music had no apparent physiological effect on the athletes, it did seem to **promote** longer exercise times, perhaps by making the athletes feel more energized or by diverting their attention from feelings of exhaustion. However, this **research contradicts** work carried out at Australia's University of Newcastle. This study **indicated** that music could improve the cardiovascular system, but that it would not necessarily lead to better athletic performance.

5   The Newcastle **research** was a continuation of a decade-long exploration of the effects of music on **physical** activity. During that decade, investigations had shown that fast-tempo music speeds up supermarket shopping, increases the chewing rates of cafeteria patrons, improves the **physical** performance of brain-injured children, and raises activity levels in architectural **drafting** rooms. Unfortunately, few studies actually addressed the question of whether music **enhances** athletic performance.

6   In the Newcastle **research**, 20 university students listened to uptempo rock music while also **visualizing** themselves performing sit-ups in a powerful manner. After this **period** of preparation, they did as many sit-ups as possible in a **brief** 30-second time span. A second group of 20 students used only **mental** imagery (no music) **prior** to their 30-second sit-up test.

7   Imagery by itself hiked heart rates by about five beats per minute during the pre-sit-up preparatory **period**, but imagery plus music increased heart rates by 20 beats per minute. However, the extra heart acceleration **induced** by rock music did not increase the number of sit-ups the students could actually perform. Each preparatory **scheme** (**visualization** alone or **visualization** plus music) boosted the total number of sit-ups by about 15 percent, compared to when no pre-sit-up strategy was **utilized**. This suggested that music added little to the powerful effect of **mental** imagery.

8   In another test, no imagery was used. Instead, 30 subjects threw darts at a target on three occasions: without music, after listening to slow **classical** music for 90 seconds, and after listening to fast rock music for 90 seconds. In the second test, music actually lowered heart rates, but had no positive effect on dart-throwing **accuracy**.

Research Conclusions

9   The Newcastle **research** suggests that music can have either a calming effect **prior** to **physical** exertion or, when combined with **appropriate** imagery, an arousing effect on the cardiovascular system. However, there is little solid evidence that either the tranquilizing or animating effect of music **promotes** superior performances when athletes listen to the music before performing. The new Connecticut **research**, however, suggests that listening to music during training sessions can indeed raise workout quality.

10   These studies provide an interesting perspective on the **role** of music and sport. **Despite** these findings, and how they are related to athletic performance, fans themselves will likely continue to embrace music, in the form of sports anthems, as a simple and entertaining way to support their teams.

Fill in the table below with three words from this article that are *not* from the AWL, but that are new for you.

Word	Part of Speech	Definition	Sample Sentence

Share your table with a partner.

Reading for Details

The following statements are incorrect. Correct them on the lines below.

1. "You'll Never Walk Alone" originally helped maintain a long tradition with Liverpool fans.

   _____

2. In the first experiment, scientists expected upbeat music to have a minimal effect on athletes.

   _____

3. In the first experiment, scientists discovered that upbeat music had serious physiological effects on athletes.

   _____

4. The University of Newcastle research indicated that music could improve the cardiovascular system as well as improve athletic performance.

   _____

5. Many studies prior to both of these have addressed the question of how music enhances athletic performance.

   _____

Share your answers with a partner. Try to use this chapter's AWL words as often as you can in your discussion.

Discussion Questions

Discuss the following questions with a partner.

1. Do you listen to music while you exercise? Why, or why not?
2. a) Reread the last sentence of paragraph 3. What do you think the phrase "statistically significant" means?
   b) What effect would a "larger sample of athletes" have on the effects of the study mentioned?
3. a) The Newcastle study discusses the use of visualization techniques. In a few sentences describe to your partner how you think this technique works.
   b) Do you ever use this technique to help you prepare for an important event (a presentation maybe, or your driver's test)? How might this technique be helpful?
4. Briefly outline (or summarize) each of the studies discussed and its results. (Keep in mind Chapter 1's points on how to summarize effectively.)
5. Refer back to this chapter's skills preview. Based on what you know about the studies discussed in the reading, which study are you more likely to trust now? Why? Discuss the positive aspects of the study you trust more, and the negative aspects of the study you trust less.

Vocabulary Practice

Definitions

Match the words below with their appropriate definitions.

1. analogy 2. scheme 3. regulate 4. despite 5. induce 6. period 7. appropriate	_____ to persuade or influence somebody to do something; to cause something; to make a woman start giving birth to her baby by giving her special drugs
	_____ a plan or system for doing or organizing something; to make secret plans to do something that will help yourself and possibly harm others
	_____ a particular length of time; having a style typical of a particular time in history; used at the end of a sentence to emphasize that there is nothing more to say about a subject
	_____ a comparison of one thing with another thing that has similar features
	_____ suitable, acceptable, or correct for the particular circumstances; to take something, somebody's ideas, etc. for your own use, especially illegally or without permission
	_____ to control something by means of rules
	_____ used to show that something happened or is true although something else might have happened to prevent it

Definitions taken or adapted from *Oxford Advanced Learner's Dictionary 8th Edition* by A. S. Hornby © Oxford University Press 2010. Reproduced by permission.

The word *period* can be a noun, adjective, or adverb. In the above definition, underline the definition of the noun, circle the definition of the adjective, and put square brackets [ ] around the adverb. Then, write a sentence below that matches each of these definitions of *period*.

1. _____

2. _____

3. _____

The word *draft* can be a noun, adjective, or verb. Write a definition for each function of the word *draft*, and provide a sample sentence for each. Use a dictionary if you need help.

1. Definition: _____

    Sentence: _____

2. Definition: _____

    Sentence: _____

3. Definition: _____

    Sentence: _____

Expanding Lexical Concepts

Collocations

Use the AWL vocabulary in the text box to form high-frequency collocations with the words below.

distinct	accurate	classic	role
aid	task	significant	promote

1. be, remain, regard as, entirely, quite _____; _____ from
2. appear, look, remain, completely, fairly, rather, relatively, statistically, deeply, extremely _____
3. starring, tragic, crucial, dominant, fundamental, pivotal, vital, traditional, conflicting, managerial, educational _____; _____ play, model, reversal
4. prove, deadly, extremely, amazingly, remarkably, surprisingly, perfectly, not quite, fairly, pretty, quite, reasonably, sufficiently _____
5. modern, all-time _____; _____ movie, novel, line
6. actively, aim / seek / try / be designed / be likely / tend to _____
7. challenging, daunting, arduous, time-consuming, dangerous, simple, mundane, tedious, complex, delicate, daily, urgent, carry out / perform / accomplish a _____
8. classroom, teaching, training, visual, hearing, walking, emergency, humanitarian, economic, food, legal, government, foreign, international, appeal / call for, grant, receive, rely on, cut, withdraw _____; _____ agency, worker, package

Using Collocations

Fill in the blanks using the AWL word in parentheses with the correct collocation from the list above. More than one answer may be suitable at times.

1. Children often use athletes as a _____ (role)
2. Natural disasters often produce large amounts of _____ (aid)
3. A single, _____ from a film can make an actor famous for decades. (classic)
4. Scientists aim to produce studies that represent _____ results in order to gain respect in their field. (significant)
5. To everyone's surprise, the song provided an _____ account of the facts. (accurate)
6. Certain advertising firms _____ their products to younger children, making efforts to post ads near elementary schools. (promote)
7. The engineers had an _____ before them—to complete the project in only two weeks.
8. Despite their physical similarities, twins often maintain _____ personality traits. (distinct)

Word Forms

Fill in the blanks with the appropriate form of the AWL vocabulary.

1. There was a clear _____ between what the two lawyers presented to the jury.
   a) contradict   b) contradictory   c) contradiction   d) contradictions

2. The exact factors contributing to the car accident remain _____.
    a) redefine   b) undefined   c) redefined   d) defining

3. Despite the tropical storm warnings, vacationers were still able to enjoy a _____
    afternoon by the pool.
    a) relaxing   b) relaxes   c) relaxation   d) relax

4. The single most important _____ for his joining the club was so that he could
    appropriate funds for his own personal use.
    a) motivate   b) motive   c) motivations   d) motives

5. The various _____ of those around him signified that they thought he was both lazy
    and unprepared.
    a) perceived   b) perceiving   c) perception   d) perceptions

6. Her job as a _____ helped secure her position in the accounting firm.
    a) statistic   b) statistics   c) statistician   d) statistical

7. Figure skaters often _____ their routine in their head numerous times before skating.
    a) visualize   b) visualization   c) visualizing   d) visually

8. Exercising _____ was once held to be an important virtue.
    a) brief   b) briefly   c) brevity   d) briefed

9. The argument was based on a _____ of the facts.
    a) interpretation   b) reinterpreted   c) misinterpretation d) misinterpret

10. One of her _____ included a little-known artist from Singapore.
    a) beneficiaries   b) benefitting   c) beneficial   d) benefited

Before Moving On...
About Beat Music

Beat music is a genre of rock and roll that has its origins in the United Kingdom, particularly in and around the city of Liverpool—a port city with close economic ties to the United States. As such, beat music was heavily influenced by American rock bands of the late 1950s, including Buddy Holly. The beat sound that emerged was a fusion of rock and roll, rhythm and blues, and soul. Beat did, however, develop its own unique sound, becoming famous in the early 1960s. Its characteristic sound centred on a combination of lead, rhythm, and bass guitars, and drums. The beat sound first found immense popularity with the Beatles, themselves from Liverpool. Gerry and the Pacemakers, also from Liverpool, found fame with this same beat rhythm.

A Music-and-Sport Song: "You'll Never Walk Alone"

About the Artists

Gerry and the Pacemakers formed in Liverpool, in 1959, following in the footsteps of the Beatles—but were never able to match the Beatles' success. Of their entire work, Gerry and the Pacemakers produced three singles that topped the UK music charts (one of them being "You'll Never Walk Alone," itself an adaptation of an original song from the 1945 musical *Carousel*), but were unable to achieve similar success in the United States. The band originally started out as Gerry Marsden and the Mars Bars, but the Mars chocolate-bar company threatened them with legal action, forcing them to change their name. The band broke up soon after its successes, in 1966, but is still well known for their hit song that was adopted by Liverpool football supporters.

Listen to the song and try to fill in the blanks. You will have two opportunities to hear it.

Gerry and the Pacemakers—"You'll Never Walk Alone"

When you walk through a storm

_____ _____ _____ _____ _____

And don't be afraid of the dark.
At the end of a storm
Is a golden sky   5
And the sweet, silver song of a _____ .
Walk on through the wind,
Walk on through the rain,
Though your dreams be _____ and _____ .
Walk on, walk on _____ _____ _____ _____ _____,   10
And you'll never walk alone!
You'll never walk alone.
Walk on, walk on _____ _____ _____ _____,
And you'll never walk alone!
You'll never walk alone.   15

To watch Liverpool fans singing this song before a game, just search for "Liverpool fans You'll Never Walk Alone" on the Internet.

Listen Again!

Listen to the song again and double-check your answers. When you are finished, check your answers with a partner.

Song Survey

In the last column provide a reason for your choice.

1. Were the lyrics easy to understand?	Yes	No	
2. Would you listen to more songs by Gerry and the Pacemakers?	Yes	No	
3. Is this the kind of song your parents would listen to?	Yes	No	
4. Do you know of another song used by fans for another team? If yes, what's the song's title or the team's name?	Yes	No	
5. Is there anything about the song you would change to make it more interesting for you and your friends? If yes, what?	Yes	No	

Share your answers with a partner.

Song Discussion

Discuss the following questions in small groups.

1. Based on the title of this song, what significance might this song have for Liverpool players and supporters?
2. Based on the lyrics of this song, what significance might this song have for Liverpool players and supporters?
3. How is the rhythm and beat of this song both similar and dissimilar to the music you listen to?

 # Focus on Speaking

Skills Focus: Thinking on Your Feet

Thinking on your feet is an idiom that expresses the ability to think quickly about a comment, question, or situation you are in. Developing this skill will help you deal with high-stress situations like a job interview, a work-related meeting, or when an instructor or classmate asks you a question in the classroom. It can even help with writing exams.

Tips in Context: Example

You have just finished talking about high-school education in your home country. After your comments you receive the following question:

> "You mentioned fixing the way high schools teach mathematics. That's an interesting concept. Can you describe what you mean by 'fix' here, in relation to schools in this country and those in your home country?"

Here are some tips to help you answer this question and develop the skill of thinking on your feet. As you will be developing this skill throughout this book, take the time to closely read the information that follows.

1. Relax
   In order for your voice to remain calm and for your brain to think, you have to be as relaxed as possible:
   - take deep breaths
   - give yourself a quick positive message ("I can do this!")
   - clench invisible muscles (thighs, biceps, feet) for a few seconds and release.

2. Listen
   Listening is critical to thinking on your feet. Why do you need to listen? This is important so that you fully understand the question before you reply. If you answer too soon, you risk talking about something that is unnecessary. To help you with your listening, remember to:
   - look directly at the questioner
   - try to interpret what is being suggested by the question or request. Is this a counter-argument to a comment you made earlier, a request for more information, or a test? Why is this person asking this and what is the intention?

   Being able to quickly process all of this is essential for mastering this skill.

3. Have the Question Repeated
   If you feel under a lot of pressure, ask for the question to be repeated. This gives you a bit more time to think about your response. Use phrases such as
   - *"I'm sorry. Could you repeat that please?"*
   - *"Excuse me, but could you say that again?"*
   - *"I'd like to hear that question again. Can you repeat that please?"*

   This is a great tactic. At first people may think this makes you look unsure. It doesn't; it makes you look concerned that you give an appropriate response. It also gives the questioner an opportunity to rephrase the question. Likely, the question will be asked in a much clearer or direct way.
   The rephrased question may look like the following: *"What kind of changes would you recommend for mathematics teachers in this country and yours?"*
   Now the question is clearer and easier for you to understand.

4. Use Tactics to Obtain More Time
   Sometimes you need more time to get your thoughts straight and calm yourself down enough to reply clearly. Do not just speak about the first thing that comes to your mind. Often this will be a defensive comment that only makes you look insecure and anxious, rather than confident and relaxed:
   - Repeat the question to yourself. This gives you time to think and clarify exactly what is being asked.
   - Narrow the focus. Here, you can ask a question of your own, not only to clarify, but to make the question easier to answer.
     - *"So, you would like to know about changes that I personally would recommend, correct?"*

5. Use Silence to Your Advantage
   We often think that silence is uncomfortable; however, use it to your advantage. It communicates that you are in control of your thoughts and confident in your ability to answer. A short, silent pause is fine.

6. Stick to One Point and One Supporting Piece of Information
   There's a high risk that, under pressure, you'll answer a question with either too much or too little information. If you give too short an answer, you risk just getting more questions. When your reply is too long, you risk losing people's interest. Remember, you are not being asked to give a speech on the subject. The questioner wants to know something. Give them an answer, with just enough supporting information. Pick one main point and one supporting fact that will allow you to answer accurately and confidently.

"Many math classes are taught by a single teacher in a lecture-style environment. Despite this style being very traditional, it's not appropriate. In the real world, we seldom isolate ourselves so much when drafting a solution to a math problem... say in building engineering. Math often requires us to coordinate with others. If math teachers used more group-centred teaching practices, students would be significantly better prepared for real-world situations. This can be done in any country." (Note the speaker's effort to use vocabulary from the AWL.)

Main point: teach group-centred math lessons
Supporting point: real-life engineering projects

> **Tip:**
> If you don't know the answer, don't be afraid to say *"Sorry, I'm not sure about that."* Don't try to make something up. You will embarrass yourself and this will lower your confidence when you need to think on your feet in the future. Be careful not to overuse this though. If you say *"Sorry, I'm not sure about that,"* after every question, your listeners will get the impression that you do not know anything about the topic.

7. Practise Clear Delivery

How you say something is almost as important as what you say. If you mumble (use "umm," "ah," or "like" between every few words), confidence in what you are saying quickly drops. Whenever you are speaking with people, make a point to practise these key oration skills:

- Speak in a strong voice (don't confuse strong with loud).
- Use pauses strategically to emphasize a point or slow yourself down.
- Use eye contact appropriately.
- Pay attention to your grammar.
- Use the level of formality that is appropriate to the situation.

8. Summarize and Stop

Finish your response with a quick summary statement. Use words like *in conclusion*, *therefore*, *finally*, or *so* to indicate to your listeners that you are about to finish.

"... If math teachers used more group-centred teaching practices, students would be better prepared for real-world situations. This can be done in any country. So / Therefore, I think this is one clear example of how math teachers can fix, or improve their classroom lessons."

After that, do not add more information. There may be silence after your answer. Do not make the common mistake of filling the silence with more information! This is the time when other people in the room are thinking about the information you have given them.

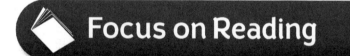

Focus on Reading

Skills Focus: Summarizing Key Points

Summarizing the key points of any text you read is an essential skill that will save you important time and energy in the future. Imagine the following situation: your psychology professor gives you 20 pages of reading material every week. After the sixth week of classes he announces an exam based on the last six weeks of reading material. If you have mastered the skill of summarizing key points, you may have only 12 pages of notes to study (2-page summaries of 20 pages of reading, for six weeks, equals about 12 pages of summary notes, for example). What about your friends who don't know how to summarize well? They'll have 120 pages to read instead! Follow these important points to master this skill:

1. Focus mainly on the key points.
2. Summarize in your own words. (This will help develop another skill you'll study in Chapter 5: paraphrasing.)

3. Pay attention to the order in which the main points are presented. (Authors usually go in a specific order for a good reason.)
4. Note the examples (often times they may help you remember ideas, points, or theories better) and the use of tables, diagrams, or statistics.
5. Provide yourself with a summary or conclusion (especially if you are reading an argument).

In the space below, summarize the reading about thinking on your feet. Do this carefully as you will be referring back to this summary throughout this book.

_____
_____
_____
_____
_____
_____
_____
_____
_____
_____
_____
_____
_____
_____
_____
_____
_____

Compare your summary with a classmate. Did you create a thorough summary? Will you understand this summary if you have to read it again in a few weeks? Make sure you've included all the key points—this will make your life less stressful in the future!

Skills in Practice

Using the above summary, prepare a short, two-part presentation. First, on the Internet, research the top 10 sports-related songs. Choose one, and prepare a brief history of the song and its artist, as well as its position relative to sports. Include your own opinion regarding this song. Second, research a song that you use for a special purpose. Does the song help you concentrate when you study? Does it motivate you when you exercise? Does it remind you of old friends, family, or experiences? Research the history of the song and the artist, and explain in detail when and why you listen to this song. As well as your own thoughts, your presentation should be a summary of your research regarding the song. Refer back to Chapter 1, pages 14 and 15, for some helpful tips on preparing an oral summary. When you are finished your presentation, be prepared to answer questions from your classmates and your instructor. Be prepared to think on your feet! Remember to keep this chapter's AWL vocabulary in mind, as well as those from the previous chapter. You should try to use as many AWL words as possible in your presentation.

Focus on Listening

Skills Focus: Lecture Note-taking Skills

A significant amount of your future education will require that you listen to instructors give lectures on any given topic. With this in mind, then, why do you think your ability to listen carefully and take accurate notes is important? Discuss this with a classmate.

Here is a list of some reasons why effective note-taking skills are important:

1. Notes often indicate the important points from the class textbook.
2. Notes will be easier to remember than the textbook.
3. Notes will provide you with a narrowed focus for later review and exam preparation.
4. Taking notes forces you to pay close attention to what your instructor is saying.

Setting Yourself Up—Some Key Points to Remember

1. Whatever system you use to take notes, stay consistent.
2. Be as brief as possible. Use a phrase instead of a sentence, a word instead of a phrase, or an abbreviation instead of a word.
3. Use margins and indentations to signify more- or less-important points.
4. Leave lots of empty space on the page (you can use it later to add any information you may have missed).
5. Don't worry if you miss something; get it from a classmate later.

What kind of abbreviations might you use while taking notes? In the space below, insert some abbreviations and what they represent. Provide an example in parentheses as well.

~	about/approximately (~ 40 kg)
⇧	increase/rise/upward (⇧ stress)

When you are finished, share your list with a partner. Below, add three new abbreviations from your partner's list.

It is also important that you do *not* try to write down everything the lecturer says. You need to be able to distinguish what needs to be in your notes, and what you can ignore. Here are some key phrases on which to focus your attention. These phrases usually signal something worth writing down.

I'll be talking about / I'm going to talk about / Let's discuss... (introduces the topic)
I'll begin / start with..., then... (introduces the outline of the lecture)
Worth noting... (introduces an important point)
Specifically / For example... (introduces an example or point of reference for clarity)
However / but / while / although... (sets up a contrasting point)
Another / Moreover / Furthermore / Okay, so... (adding an important point to a previous one)
First / First of all... (setting up a list of points)
Who / what / where / when / why... (rhetorical questions used to begin a new topic or bring up a new point)
Finally / In conclusion / Lastly... (signals the end of a point or topic)

Also, pay attention to any definitions that are given or any numbers or statistics that are used. Finally, if your instructor writes something on the board or provides a visual cue, it is probably important. Instructors won't waste their time with these unless they are important.

Skills in Practice

Track 1: The Music of Language and the Language of Music

You are about to listen to the beginning of a lecture on how the brain interacts with music. The lecture is entitled "The Music of Language and the Language of Music." It is delivered by Professor Aniruddh Patel, from The Neurosciences Institute in Southern California. The first time you listen, pay attention only to the words or phrases the lecturer uses that might signal something worth writing down. Make a list of these words and / or phrases as you listen. There are about 15. When you are finished, share your list with a partner.

_____	_____	_____
_____	_____	_____
_____	_____	_____
_____	_____	_____
_____	_____	_____

Pre-listening Vocabulary

tribe (noun): a group of people of the same race, and with the same customs, language, religion, etc., living in a particular area
empirical (noun): based on experiments or experience rather than ideas or theories

Definitions taken or adapted from *Oxford Advanced Learner's Dictionary 8th Edition* by A. S. Hornby © Oxford University Press 2010. Reproduced by permission.

Quickly review the points listed for effective note-taking. Then, listen to the lecture again and take notes. The images on the following page are of slides used during the lecture. Refer to them when the lecturer does.

Some similarities	But . . .

• Rhythm
  - Systematic patterns of timing, accent, grouping
 	
• Melody
  - Structured patterns of pitch over time
 	
• Syntax
  - Discrete elements + principles of combination
 	
• Affect
	• Rhythm
	  - A sustained pulse
	
	• Melody What's new:
	  - Stable pitch intervals Empirical studies
	
	• Syntax
	  - Propositional semantics
	
	• Affect
	  - Musical vs. everyday emotions

When you are finished, compare your notes with some classmates and get from them any information you may have missed. When you are done turn to page 183 in the Appendix. Compare your notes with the model provided there.

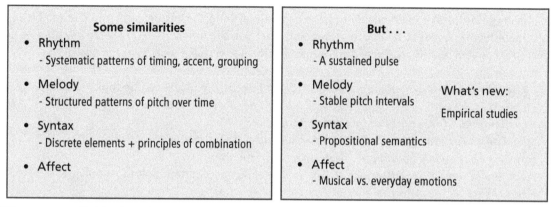

Focus on Writing

Skills Focus: The Writing Process—Developing a Thesis Statement

Your essays are never merely a casual discussion about a topic. Instead, your papers usually have a clear purpose, whether to focus on a certain idea, argue a specific point, compare ideas, describe something in detail, or argue an opinion. A thesis statement provides a central focus for your essay. A poorly written thesis statement, or no thesis statement at all, will likely result in a poorly organized and poorly written paper. Your thesis is your guiding point for the entire writing process. As such, it must be extremely clear (likely the clearest sentence in your entire paper).

The topic you are writing about is *not* your thesis statement; don't confuse the two. A topic is usually quite broad. Your thesis statement, however, is the opposite—very narrow. It is very specific and indicates the entire point, or focus, of your paper. Look at the following example:

Essay Question: Discuss the factors involved in the increase of hearing loss of Americans today.

Topic (vague): Sound and hearing in American youth

Less vague: Influence of sound and hearing problems in American youth

More focused: Influence of music on hearing in American teenagers

Focused and clear: American male teens: how loud music can cause hearing loss

After beginning with a vague topic, narrow it down into one, central, and highly focused area. Now, you need to construct the thesis statement. What will you argue in your paper? Your thesis statement needs to tell your reader *exactly* what you will discuss. Here are some possible thesis statements for the topic above:

- The popularity of high-quality headphones among male American teenagers is creating serious health concerns that are affecting the nation's youth.
- The rise of hand-held entertainment devices among American male teenagers is leading to serious hearing problems that need to be addressed immediately.
- Companies that promote audio entertainment should be held accountable for hearing problems in many of today's American male teenagers.

Each of these statements makes a clear point. Each tells the reader exactly what they can expect the essay to be about. Each of these is a single sentence, and expresses an opinion that the writer will defend in the essay. Here are some tips to keep in mind when writing a thesis statement:

- Clarity: A thesis statement makes a *clear* claim regarding a topic; there is an actual point of view or opinion expressed that needs to be defended.
- Brevity: A thesis statement should be stated in a single sentence.
- Location: In general, it is the last sentence of your introduction (though this isn't always the case).

Below is a list of common errors students make when writing a thesis statement. Study them.

1. The thesis statement consists of an empty observation, rather than making an assertion.
2. The thesis statement is underdeveloped and vague, and needs to be made more specific and narrower.
3. The thesis statement exceeds the scope of the essay; i.e., it is too broad to be discussed thoroughly.
4. The thesis statement is too detailed or wordy. The arguments should be summarized in the introduction and developed in subsequent paragraphs.
5. The thesis statement introduces several unrelated points, rather than the main points of the argument.

Match each error type above with an example of it from the list below (note that there may be more than one possible answer). When you are finished use the lines below each example to write a *clear* and focused thesis statement.

_____ Universal health care should be enjoyed by everyone, the price of vegetables will increase with global warming, and the education system needs to be fixed soon.

_____

_____

_____ Long winters can create psychological problems for some people.

_____

_____

_____ The Amazon River, the second-longest river in the world, can provide 935 litres of water for people, 855 litres for animals, and 700 litres for plants every 10 minutes because the strength of the river's flow constantly pushes out so much water.

_____

_____

_____ This paper will discuss economic problems in Brazil.

_____

_____

_____ Specific foods may allow people to live longer.

_____

_____

Skills in Practice

◎ Develop a thesis statement for each of the essay topics below. To do so, you will have to think critically about each topic first. What important ideas do you want to express and defend regarding each question?

1. Examine how music is adapted by different parts of society to create popular sub-cultures.
2. Describe the benefits of extra-curricular activities for students.
3. Discuss the importance of not driving under the influence of alcohol.
4. Critique the following quotation: "Libraries are no longer needed because the Internet has more information that any library does."
5. Discuss the consequences to society of exposing young children to horror movies.

Additional Vocabulary

Word	Part of Speech	Definition	Sample Sentence

Chapter 3

Tragedies at Sea

Introduction

◎ Match the tragic events listed below in the left column with their death tolls, listed on the right. When you are finished share your answers with a partner. Are they the same? Discuss the reasons behind your choices. Finally, how many of these tragic events do you know something about? What, if anything, do you know about them?

Tragic Event

1. _____ Indian Ocean Tsunami (2004)
2. _____ Haiti Earthquake (2010)
3. _____ World War II military deaths (1939–1945)
4. _____ AIDS-related deaths (daily)
5. _____ RMS *Titanic* cruise ship (1912)
6. _____ Space Shuttle *Columbia* (2003)
7. _____ Malnutrition / hunger-related deaths (daily)

Death Tolls
(all numbers are approximate)

a) 25,000,000
b) 22,000
c) 7
d) 225,000
e) 5500
f) 1517
g) 230,000

A home in Banda Aceh, Indonesia destroyed by the 2004 Tsunami

The Space Shuttle *Columbia*

◎ With a partner compare the number of deaths. Should these numbers represent how much media coverage these events receive? Which types of events or deaths are you most likely to hear about on the news or in the media in general? Why?

Previewing the Reading

As readers, each of us approaches reading material with a different background, a background formed by various experiences and histories. Sharing, or discussing what we already know with others, activates our minds and can prepare us for what we are about to read. In small groups, discuss your experiences with relation to the questions below. Take turns going around your group sharing your ideas.

1. Have you ever been in severe weather (thunderstorm, typhoon, etc.)? How did it make you feel?
2. What is the closest near-death or traumatic experience you have ever had? What happened? How did you handle the situation?

3. Have you ever helped someone in need? If so, describe how you helped them.
4. What is the biggest *natural* threat to the lives of the people in your home country? (For example, people living in Florida are often threatened by hurricanes; poisonous snakes might be dangerous for people living in rural Australia.) Share any stories you might have regarding this question.

⟳ Tragedies at Sea

Academic Word List (AWL) Vocabulary

The following AWL words will appear in this chapter's reading. Before completing the exercise below skim the reading with a focus on the words in bold print. This will help you complete the table below, and will prepare you for the reading.

facilitate	commission	ambiguous	contact
constitute	estimate	sufficient	intense
impact	function	communicate	capacity
grant	assure	route	establish
transfer	identify	previous	impose
somewhat	trace	amend	chart
conduct	proceed	issue	locate
section	reject	inspect	consent
scope	label	status	instruct
constrain			

Place each of the above vocabulary words under the appropriate heading in the chart below. Use a dictionary if you need help.

Noun & Verb		Verb		Adjective	Noun	Adverb

Tragedies at Sea at a Glance...

1   The *Oxford Advanced Learner's Dictionary* defines *legend* as "a story from ancient times about people and events, that may or may not be true." Legends have been a part of humankind's oral history for thousands of years. The following is a true story based on an Aboriginal legend that **instructed** people to avoid *Gitche Gumee* (the Chippewa name for Lake Superior) during

November for fear of drowning. While the event itself is factual, numerous theories remain unanswered regarding the ship's final minutes, helping to **constitute** the ship's legendary **status**.

Background Information

2   On 8 November 1975, in the American state of Oklahoma, the beginnings of a storm stirred the air. Picking up force, the storm moved through Iowa and Wisconsin. On November 9, gale warnings were **issued** for Lake Superior. By the time the storm had **established** itself over Lake Superior, the American Meteorological Association had **labelled** it a cyclone.

3   By mid-afternoon on November 9, a giant shipping freighter had **transferred** 26,000 tons of land-based iron into its cargo hold. It then **proceeded** perilously to cross Lake Superior on its way south to Detroit. That vessel was the *Edmund Fitzgerald*.

The *Edmund Fitzgerald*, August 1975

4   The *Edmund Fitzgerald* was christened on 8 June 1958 and launched on June 17 into the Detroit River. A life-insurance company had **commissioned** it to be built by Great Lakes Engineering Works. It took an **estimated** 1000 employees to complete the project. At 222 metres long, it was at that time the largest freighter on the Great Lakes. With a depth of 12 metres, it had a load **capacity** of almost 30,000 tons.

5   By 1975, the *Fitzgerald* was showing an average amount of wear for a ship on the Great Lakes. It had passed a rigorous two-month **inspection** (**conducted** yearly) in the spring of 1975, and had passed a periodical coast-guard out-of-water **inspection** in the spring of 1974. It was certified as seaworthy and safe for operation. An October 31 **inspection identified** routine seasonal damage to the cargo hatches, but the *Fitzgerald* was still deemed **functional**, and was **granted consent** to operate as long as the repairs were complete before the 1976 shipping season.

6   There were 29 men aboard on that November day, captained by Ernest McSorley, 63. High water in the lakes since 1969 had prompted the US Coast Guard to remove **previous constraints**, allowing owners to load their ships to a greater depth, and the *Fitzgerald* was no exception. It was loaded one metre deeper than had been considered safe in 1969, thus bringing

her deck one metre closer to the water line.

The Fateful Journey

7   The *Fitzgerald* came within 32 kilometres of the vessel *Arthur M. Anderson*, near Two Harbors, Minnesota. The *Anderson* was also loaded with iron. The two captains **communicated** by radio, discussing the aforementioned storm's increasing **intensity**, and at 2:00 AM Monday, the morning of the tenth,

A map of the Great Lakes

they decided to **amend** their course and take the northern route along Lake Superior's north shore. This would put them in the lee of the Canadian shoreline, which hopefully would provide **sufficient** protection from the gale-force winds that were whipping up the lake waters.

8   At 7:00 AM Captain McSorley **contacted** his company to report that weather would delay their arrival. The *Anderson* was following the *Fitzgerald* at a distance of nearly 25 kilometres and keeping in **contact**. Winds were high, and getting worse. Waves were 3 metres in the early afternoon and increasing in power and size as the day wore on. The *Fitzgerald* soon lost the **function** of both its radars. The *Arthur M. Anderson* was asked to guide the *Edmund Fitzgerald*.

9   As heavy snow began to fall, visibility became nil and the *Fitzgerald* disappeared from the *Anderson's* view. Waves reached almost 5 metres, whipped up by winds gusting up to 150 kilometres per hour at some **locations**. The coast guard **issued** an

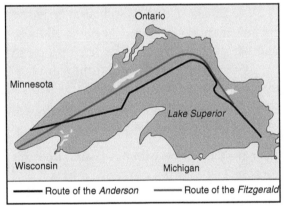

The routes of the *Anderson* and *Fitzgerald*

emergency warning: all ships were to find safe harbour. By 6:00 PM the crashing waves were 7.5 metres high.

10   According to the *Anderson's* captain, the *Fitzgerald* passed closer to the Caribou Island's Six-Fathom Shoal than he would have taken his own vessel.

The End is Near

11 At 7:10 PM the Anderson radioed the *Fitzgerald* to warn of another vessel 14 kilometres ahead, but **assured** McSorley that on present course the ship would pass safely by to the west. The first mate of the *Arthur M. Anderson* signed off by asking, "How are you making out with your problem?"

        "We are holding our own," the *Fitzgerald* replied.

        It was the last **communication** with the ship.

12   The snow was letting up and the Anderson crew began sighting other ships. None were the *Fitzgerald*. The 222-metre mammoth was missing.

13   A search was launched. Aircraft and patrol boats **facilitated** the search, and the *Arthur M. Anderson* turned around to help. The *Anderson* discovered a piece of one of the *Fitzgerald's* lifeboats. A life preserver was found, as well as another lifeboat, a raft, and a stepladder. The search continued for three days, but no bodies were recovered and hardly any **trace** of the huge ore carrier remained.

14   Down in Detroit on Tuesday morning, the bell at Mariners' Church tolled 29 times, once for each of the lost crew.

15   On November 14 an American military plane **located** the wreck. The full **scope** of the disaster was now being realized. It was just 27 kilometres from its safe harbour destination of Whitefish Point. The vessel was in two huge **sections** 161 metres down on the bottom of Lake Superior, the metal torn and twisted, supposedly from the force of the **impact**.

The Cause

16   There was never a definitive report on the cause of the *Fitzgerald* wreck. A coast-guard report suggesting that the hatches had not been closed properly was **rejected**. Popular speculation held that in passing so close to the Caribou Island shoal, the extra weight of the ship caused the hull to scrape the shoals, whose depth was misreported on navigational **charts** at the time. Some believe that the towering rolling waves caused the steamer to break in two. However, with the ship sitting in 161 metres of water, these theories still remain **somewhat ambiguous**.

17   The *Edmund Fitzgerald* will never be raised, nor its crew recovered. It remains an underwater monument not only to its crew but to all those who sail the Great Lakes, a monument to courage and the spirit of adventure that leads people to the sea.

18   Within this tragic story rests the legend of Gitche Gumee—a vast, **imposing** expanse of open water unwilling to surrender its visitors when November gales rage. It is from such beliefs that legends are strengthened, and it is about this tragic event that Gordon Lightfoot wrote "The Wreck of the Edmund Fitzgerald."

Fill in the table below with three words from this article that are *not* from the AWL, but that are new for you.

Word	Part of Speech	Definition	Sample Sentence

Share your table with a partner.

Reading for Details

The following statements are incorrect. Correct them on the lines below.

1. Due to a decrease in water levels, ships on the Great Lakes were allowed to increase the load of their cargo.

2. The *Fitzgerald* was asked to guide the *Anderson* because its radars no longer functioned properly.

_____

3. Both the *Anderson* and the *Fitzgerald* passed close to the Caribou Island Six-Fathom Shoal.

_____

4. In 161 metres of water, the *Edmund Fitzgerald* was found intact.

_____

Share your answers with a partner. Try to use this chapter's AWL vocabulary as often as you can.

Discussion Questions

Discuss the following questions with a partner.

1. a) Reread paragraph 10, and then study the map indicating the course of the two ships. Where might Caribou Island Six-Fathom Shoal be on the map? Further, based on information from the reading, why do you think the captain of the *Anderson* avoided this area?
   b) What speculation arose from the *Fitzgerald*'s decision to take an alternative route to the *Anderson* regarding Caribou Island?
2. Which of the three theories explaining the sinking of the *Fitzgerald*, outlined in the third-last paragraph, do you think is most plausible? Why? Defend your position with clear reasons.

Vocabulary Practice

Definitions

Match the words below with their appropriate definitions.

Words	Definitions
1. somewhat	_____ enough for a particular purpose; as much as you need
2. constrain	_____ to change a law, document, statement, etc. slightly in order to correct a mistake or to improve it
3. sufficient	
4. facilitate	_____ that can be understood in more than one way; having different meanings; not clearly stated or defined
5. amend	
6. ambiguous	_____ the opportunity or ability to do or achieve something; the range of things that a subject, an organization, an activity, etc. deals with; an instrument for looking through or watching something with; to look at or examine something thoroughly
7. scope	
8. consent	
	_____ to force somebody to do something or behave in a particular way; to restrict or limit somebody / something
	_____ to a moderate extent or by a moderate amount
	_____ permission to do something, especially given by somebody in authority; agreement about something; an official document giving permission for something; to agree to something or give your permission for something
	_____ to make an action or a process possible or easier

Definitions taken or adapted from *Oxford Advanced Learner's Dictionary 8th Edition* by A. S. Hornby © Oxford University Press 2010. Reproduced by permission.

Expanding Lexical Concepts

Collocations

Use the AWL vocabulary in the text box to form high-frequency collocations with the words below.

capacity	commission	function
status	impose	trace
impact	issue	contact
grant		

1. private, international, joint, independent, government, planning, establish / set up / chair / earn / receive a, small, fixed _____

2. important, useful, vital, chief, primary, bodily, charity, official, carry out / fulfill / hold / attend a, _____; _____ effectively, efficiently, successfully, properly, adequately, independently

3. have close / regular / direct, come into, establish, get / keep in, maintain, break off, lose, business, physical, sexual, come into _____; _____ immediately, directly, personally, by email / phone / telephone

4. superior, inferior, equal, current, special, economic, employment, financial, marital, legal, immigrant, refugee, legendary, enjoy, acquire _____; _____ symbol, quo

5. effectively, seek / strive / try to _____; _____ on, upon, restrictions

6. permanent, leave / reveal / discover a, disappear without, discernible, faint, minute, attempt / unable / fail to, historically, _____; _____ amount

7. considerable, enormous, profound, significant, limited, negligible, immediate, short- / long-term, lasting, human, economic, emotional, environmental, have an, make an, cushion the, minimize the _____

8. limited, maximum, total, productive, earning, seating, storage, engine, lung, packed to, increase, expand, reduce, work at full, innate, intellectual, beyond / within one's, official, unofficial, private _____

9. burning, central, critical, important, key, wider, side, fundamental, contentious, controversial, thorny, domestic, global, environmental, ethical, raise / debate / discuss / address / deal with / examine / explore / highlight / avoid an / the _____; _____ formally, jointly, immediately

10. emergency, student, research, government, apply / be eligible / qualify for a, decide / refuse to, receive a _____; _____ permission, approval, parole

Using Collocations

Fill in the blanks using the AWL word in parentheses with the correct collocation from the list above. More than one answer may be suitable at times.

1. The committee members refused to _____ despite having contacted the main parties involved. (issue)

2. Her endless work for children in the developing world had an _____ on communities throughout central Africa. (impact)

3. The _____ of university graduates varies according to what kind of degree they graduate with. (capacity)

4. Travellers _____ with dengue fever or malaria should seek immediate medical attention. (contact)

5. Luxury goods companies such as Gucci and Rolex continue to maintain their image as a _____ throughout most of the world. (status)

6. Both his wife and child _____ shortly after lunch; it was the last time he ever saw them. (trace)

7. A _____ was held last night, although where the humanitarian aid will go still remains somewhat ambiguous. (function)

8. After weeks of hearings, the judge refused to _____ to those who had helped facilitate the murder. (grant)

9. Tyrannous governments often try to _____ upon the freedom of its citizens. (impose)

10. A _____ was set up between Canada and the United Kingdom to investigate the failure of both governments to secure its borders. (commission)

Word Forms

Fill in the blanks with the appropriate form of the AWL vocabulary.

1. Most of those eligible in her _____ voted in favour of the latest proposal.
   a) constitution   b) constituent   c) constituents   d) constituency

2. The manager _____ the ability of the new employee to facilitate the discussion.
   a) underestimated   b) overestimate   c) estimation   d) estimating

3. It was the police officer's _____ to release the elderly lady with only a warning.
   a) intensification   b) intensity   c) intensively   d) intention

4. _____ letters are often damaging to one's self-esteem.
   a) Rejecting   b) Rejection   c) Reject   d) Rejections

5. Without any _____ features it was impossible to accurately distinguish one character from another.
   a) identifiable   b) unidentifiable   c) identified   d) identities

6. Law students are often asked to pay careful attention to _____ that deal with the focus of their studies.
   a) procedural   b) proceedings   c) proceeds   d) procedural

7. Attaining _____ competency is a common goal of students learning a new language.
   a) communicable   b) communicating   c) communicative   d) communication

8. The task of carrying out various _____ based on formal complaints is somewhat time consuming.
   a) inspections   b) inspectors   c) inspection   d) inspects

9. His parents are antique dealers, and as such often prefer a more traditional _____ in which to dine.
   a) established   b) disestablish   c) establishment   d) disestablishment

10. The developer gave them his _____ that his commission for the project would fall well within the range of what they had agreed to.
    a) assured   b) assuring   c) assurance   d) assures

Before Moving On...

About Folk Music

Folk music was discussed earlier in Chapter 1. What do you remember about it? Answer the following questions with a partner:

1. When did the term *folk music* originate?
2. What is unique about the lyrics of folk music?
3. What are some traditional folk music instruments?
4. When did folk music re-emerge in the last century as a popular form of music?

♫ A Tragedies-at-Sea Song: "The Wreck of the *Edmund Fitzgerald*"

About the Artist

Gordon Lightfoot has been a mainstay of the Canadian music scene since the 1960s. His deep baritone voice and acoustic guitar sound are easily identifiable as Lightfoot-esque. The singer-songwriter was born in a small town north of Toronto, Canada, in 1938. Comfortable playing the guitar or piano, or singing, his work crosses three genres: rock, country, and folk. Gifted as a songwriter, Lightfoot's work has been covered by various artists who represent vastly different musical styles. Musicians who have recorded Lightfoot's work include Bob Dylan, Elvis Presley, Sarah McLachlan, and garage-rock band The Dandy Warhols. Along with Leonard Cohen, Lightfoot is considered by many as one of Canada's greatest songwriters.

Follow the directions below. You will have at least two opportunities to hear the song and complete the exercise.

Unlike Chapters 1 and 2, this is not a fill-in-the-blanks exercise. Instead, on the right side of the table you will try to write the main idea(s) expressed in each stanza (note too that each stanza has been broken into two parts). You will need to write quickly, as you are developing the speed at which you organize your thoughts and put them to paper. You're not trying to just copy what the singer says. You are trying to capture the part of the story that the singer is trying to express. Some key words for each stanza are provided as a guiding point for your ideas, as are the beginning lyrics of each section.

The first one has been done for you. After you listen to the first stanza (the first 52 seconds) study how the example was done, and then begin again.

Song Vocabulary

Chippewa (noun): member of a Native American people, many of whom live in the US states of Michigan, Wisconsin, and Minnesota and in Ontario in Canada
Gitche Gumee (noun): Chippewa name for Lake Superior

Gordon Lightfoot—"The Wreck of the *Edmund Fitzgerald*"

Stanza	Keywords	Stanza Summary
1a	The legend explained ("The legend...")	- a Chippewa legend of the lake - lake always kills when Nov. skies are bad
1b	Edmund Fitzgerald fact ("With a load...")	- E.F. 26,000 tons heavier than when empty
2a	The ship and crew ("The shop...")	
2b	The destination and an omen ("Concluding some terms...")	
3a	The first sign of a storm ("The wind...")	
3b	The storm conditions ("The dawn...")	
4a	The cook speaks ("When supper-time...")	
4b	The captain speaks ("The captain...")	
5a	The search team speaks ("Does anyone...")	
5b	Theories of how the ship sunk ("They might have...")	
6a	Lakes Huron, Superior, and Michigan ("Lake Huron...")	
6b	Lakes Ontario and Erie ("And farther...")	
7a	Prayers and Bells ("In a musty...")	
7b	The legend of Lake Superior ("The legend...")	

Listen Again!

Listen to the song again and double-check your answers. If necessary listen a third time. When you are finished, check your answers with a partner.

Song Survey

In the last column, provide a reason for your choice.

1. Were the lyrics easy to understand?	Yes	No	
2. Would you listen to more songs by Gordon Lightfoot?	Yes	No	
3. Is this the kind of song your parents would listen to?	Yes	No	
4. Now that you know the background story to this song, would you recommend it to your friends?	Yes	No	
5. Do you know of other songs that are about a specific event such as this one? If yes, what is the song about?	Yes	No	

Share your answers with a partner.

Song Discussion

Discuss the following questions in small groups.

1. Line 9 says that this ship was "the pride of the American side"? Why might this be the case?
2. Compare the song lyrics and the reading. How accurate are the lyrics compared to the event described in the reading? What details are in both the song and the reading? And what details are left out of each?
3. Share a legend or a legendary event from your own culture (remember that it need not be factual).

Focus on Reading

Skills Review: Stylistic Analysis

Do an Internet search for the lyrics to "The Wreck of the *Edmund Fitzgerald*," and find an example of each literary device listed below. Indicate the line numbers as well for easy referencing. (Definitions for the parts of speech and literary devices below can be found in Chapter 1, pages 16–17.)

1. Abstract noun

   _____

2. Non-gradable adjective

   _____

3. Assonance

   _____

4. Synecdoche

_____

5. Personification

_____

6. Poetic licence

_____

7. Rhetorical question

_____

◎ Skills Focus: Evaluating Sources of Information

Today, because of the Internet, research is often performed online, and there is now an enormous amount of information available to you. The Internet may be the most convenient place to begin your research, but it is not always the best.

Internet and Print Sources—Understanding the Difference

Being able to evaluate sources of information is an essential skill for academic success. Much of this is like detective work—you have to decide where to look, what clues to search for, and what to accept. You may be overwhelmed with too much information and the temptation is to accept whatever you find. But don't be tempted. College and university instructors expect that you are able to know, for example, if something is written by a professional in the field or by a high school student with Internet access.

Many sources, such as newspapers or academic journals, are available on the Internet and in print format. Printed material usually has a digital equivalent, but very little of what you find on the Internet is available in print format. This raises a serious problem for students and academics, because material on the Internet often does not have a very high standard for publication. Consider the material outlined in the table below. It will help you understand the differences between print and Internet sources, and will help guide you in selecting appropriate sources for your studies. As you work through the table add your own ideas where you see a space. This will help you think more deeply about some of the key differences between print and Internet sources, and should help you make sound decisions regarding your own research in the future (and for this chapter's writing assignment too).

Category	Print	Internet
Getting Published	• multiple steps before publication • numerous professional reviewers and editors check the material for quality •	• if you have Internet access, you can publish anything you want • not required to have anyone review your material or check your facts •
The Author(s)	• a brief biography of the author is usually provided • authors are usually qualified professionals in their field of interest •	• author's name is often not listed • author could be a doctor, or a high school student. Often this information is not made available, and even when it is, it may be hard to verify. •

Citations	• easy to find references • bibliography almost always included • they are usually of other professional works in the field of study •	• authors here can choose to omit citations, or not clearly mark when they use them •
Favouritism	• often neutral as publishers are interested in making money (favouring one interest group will likely not generate a big enough profit)	• hard to identify purpose of publication (may be supporting a political group, or may have been sponsored by a private company)
Publication Facts	• date of publication, publishing company, and author are clearly noted	• difficult to determine date of publication (the material may be old) • if dates are listed, they may be difficult to interpret (is it the date of the site's most recent update or the day it was posted?)

 # Focus on Writing

Skills Focus: Writing a Persuasive Essay

Remember that a persuasive essay generally follows a set pattern (there are, of course, other variations). You should try to follow it in your writing.

- introduction (includes your thesis statement—usually the last sentence)
- first reason for your argument
    - support for the first reason
- second reason for your argument
    - support for the second reason
- third reason for your argument
    - support for the third reason
- counter-argument (most important reason of your opponents)
- refutation (your reason why your opponents are wrong)
    Note that counter-arguments and refutations will be dealt with in detail in chapters 8 and 9.
- conclusion (restating your thesis statement and a summary of your reasons)

Note that the support you use for each reason will usually come in the form of material you find on the Internet or in a library.

Skills in Practice

Reread paragraph 16 of this chapter's reading. Three possible explanations are given for why the *Edmund Fitzgerald* sank. Write a persuasive (argumentative) essay that supports one of these theories. Combine what you have learned thus far about developing a thesis statement (Chapter 2, pages 36–37), and supporting your claims with evidence (Chapter 1, pages 17–19) to convince your reader of the most likely acceptable theory. Whereas in Chapter 1 your argument was supported by material from the song (the lyrics), here your argument will have to be supported by external source material, from both the Internet and print media. Use the skills you studied in Focus on Reading (Evaluating Sources of Information) to help you determine which sources of information will most strengthen your argument.

Follow the pattern for a persuasive essay discussed on the previous page; your essay should be at least six paragraphs long.

🎧 Focus on Listening

Skills Focus: Listening for Cause and Effect

The relationship between cause and effect is sometimes simple to identify. The cause of a beautiful flower, for example, may be the right amount of water and an ideal temperature; i.e., perfect weather conditions create (cause) lovely flowers (effect). At other times, however, identifying this link may not be as easy—especially when listening to something. (With reading you can go back and read the material again and again, until you understand it; with listening, however, you often get only one chance—hence one reason for the increase in difficulty.) The use of cause-and-effect reasoning is ubiquitous in English. Look, for example, at the newspaper headlines below.

1. Hurricane Hits—12 Dead	3. Downtown Celebrates Cubs' Victory
2. Lottery Winner Gives All to Charity	4. Consumer Confidence Up with Employment Numbers

With a partner discuss what the cause is for each, and the effect.

In this chapter you will be practising how to identify the relationship between cause and effect. Understanding this relationship will allow you to understand how material is organized: Are comparisons being made? Is there a contrast? Does a pattern exist? Is a sequence of events being depicted? Also, understanding how others organize their ideas will help you organize your own when you are listening, writing, and speaking.

Skills in Practice

Track 2: Bermuda Triangle

Listen to a brief audio clip regarding the Bermuda Triangle. The Bermuda Triangle is an area of water filled with intrigue and mystery.

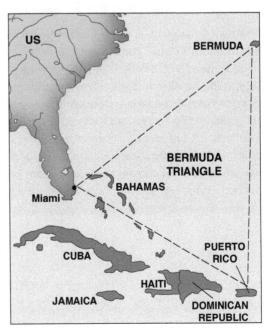

The location of the Bermuda Triangle

Boats and airplanes are often reported missing (and never recovered) from this patch of the Atlantic Ocean. Numerous theories exist as to why objects disappear here, but a clear, satisfactory explanation has yet to be found.

Cause	Effect
Unexplained disappearance of boats and aircrafts	Bermuda Triangle becomes infamous
A result of all the mystery	Term "Bermuda Triangle" synonymous with any unexplained disappearance
Nothing unusual about this area with similar weather (it's not dangerous)	
	Triggers myth of Bermuda Triangle
	Loss of military aircrafts
Instructor of first plane feels uneasy or ill	
Instructing pilot not wearing a watch	
	Conspiracy theories emerged concerning the two flights

1. Study the table above, and then listen to the entire piece (do not take notes), and familiarize yourself with the format of the talk.
2. Listen a second time and make any necessary notes to help you fill in the table above. (The first two have been done for you.)
3. Listen again for a third time. When you are finished compare your table with a partner.
4. After you have compared your tables, listen again. Review your notes and make changes or additions if you need to.

 # Focus on Speaking

Skills Focus: Research Presentations

In formal, academic settings you will often be asked to present your research to a small group or an entire class. Much of what you are doing is providing a summary of your findings. In this chapter you will focus on two specific skills: using appropriate phraseology and the presentation form.

Each academic discipline will have its own high-frequency words. For example, the word *conscience* would be used more frequently in psychology than it would be in mathematics. There are, however, certain expressions that you can use in any academic setting. Furthermore, most presentations will follow a similar format. You are already quite familiar with this format, as it resembles that of an essay: introduction, body, and conclusion. Study the table on the next page. It includes information about the structure of your presentation, as well as appropriate expressions for each section. (Wherever you see a blank line, insert one of your own examples.)

Presentation Section	Explanation	Appropriate Expressions or Phraseology
I. Introduction • indicate *what* you will talk about	• introduce your topic	What I'd like to do is to discuss… What I intend to do is to explain… I'd like to elaborate on… Today, I'm going to talk about… Today I want to consider… In this talk, I will concentrate on… The purpose of this talk is…
• indicate how you will do so	• outline the format your presentation will take	I'm going to deal with three aspects of… I've divided my presentation into three sections. I thought it would be useful to divide my talk into three sections. This subject can be looked at under the following three headings: … I'll take about *X* minutes to discuss… I'll be happy to answer questions at the end…
II. Body • explain the argument and evidence that you collected	• begin with your thesis or hypothesis (what you are trying to prove or explain) and then logically move through your argument (providing visuals [graphs, charts, photographs, etc.] if necessary)	Using the proper expressions in the body depends on what you are discussing. For example: 1. Sequencing: To start / begin with… First of all… Secondly… Next… Lastly… Finally… 2. Examples: For example / instance… As proof of that… 3. Emphasizing a Point: Furthermore… What's more… This supports my argument that… It follows, therefore, that… 4. Back Referencing: As I said at the beginning… In the first part of my talk, I noted… As I mentioned earlier… Earlier I mentioned…

		5. Rewording: In other words... That is to say... To put it another way... The point I'm making is... What I'm suggesting is...
		6. Visuals: Let's have a look at... I'd like you to look at... If you turn your attention to... I'd like to draw your attention to... The graph illustrates... As you can see... If you look closely, you'll see...
		7. Moving On: I'd now like to move on to... Turning now to... Moving on to... Having looked at..., I'd now like to consider... Now, let's turn to... Another interesting point is... The next aspect I'd like to consider is...
III. Conclusion	• provide a brief summary of your main points and restate what you have proven or uncovered with your research	We've seen that... First, we looked at... and saw that... Then we considered... and I argued... In brief, we have looked at... To sum up then... In conclusion, I'd like to emphasize that... That completes my presentation. Thank you for your attention.
	• answer any questions	If you have any comments or questions, I'd be happy to hear them. Would anyone like to make a comment, or ask a question? I'd be glad to try and answer any questions.

◎ Skills in Practice

In the essay you wrote earlier in the chapter, you created an argument that was supported by evidence that your research uncovered. Present what you found to a small group. Note that when you present your research you should *not* be just reading your paper, you should be making separate notes that deal with the highlights of your research. If you just read your paper, your presentation will be uninteresting. Your classmates may fall asleep. Your instructor will not be happy. Your grade will be poor. And worst of all, your speaking skills will not improve (plus, no one in the professional world just reads a presentation—such presentations are considered to be of very low quality). Be sure to present it in a formal academic style, as outlined on the previous pages. Also, review Chapter 2's lesson Thinking on Your Feet (pages 30–32). This will help you answer any questions you may receive after your presentation.

Additional Vocabulary

Word	Part of Speech	Definition	Sample Sentence

Chapter 4

Bloody Sunday

Introduction

What kind of situation might these photos be depicting? Use the photos and the words below to create a story that describes what is happening, and the reasons for these actions. Tell your story to a partner or small group.

anxiety	injustice	religion	unemployment	death
poverty	history	protest	gunfire	politics

Previewing the Reading

You are about to read about Bloody Sunday, an important event in the history of Europe. Before you do so, read the following related newspaper headlines and clippings. Use this exercise as an opportunity to preview the reading, that is, to build context for this chapter's reading.

1. "Events in recent weeks have shown there is something radically wrong in Northern Ireland, and it is time something was done about it."
2. Thirteen killed as paratroops break riot
3. Thirty years on, the wound is still open
4. "I regret to report that, if you want a house in the town of Dungannon, Co. Tyrone, your chances will depend to a great extent on what church you belong to."
5. Increase in violence. In the three years prior to Bloody Sunday, 210 were killed in troubles. In the 11 months after Bloody Sunday 445 people lost their lives.
6. Bloody Sunday "still unclear"
7. "That is it: there isn't any solution now."
8. "Unless the discrimination issue is faced honestly there can be no worthwhile future either for Protestant or Catholic in Northern Ireland."
9. Rocky road to rebuilding trust

According to the information in these headlines and clippings, categorize the events according to the chart below. Look for clues to help you, and make inferences whenever necessary.

	Headline and/or Clipping Numbers
Reported in the news *prior to* Bloody Sunday	_____ _____ _____
Reported in the news *soon after* Bloody Sunday	_____ _____ _____
Reported in the news *years after* Bloody Sunday	_____ _____ _____

Share your answers with a partner.

After the headlines and clippings have been categorized sequentially, reread them.

a) What kind of information is provided?
b) What do you expect to read about in this chapter?
c) What do you think happened on Bloody Sunday?

◎ Discuss with a partner.

ⓐ Bloody Sunday

Academic Word List (AWL) Vocabulary

The following AWL words will appear in this chapter's reading. Before completing the following exercise, skim the reading with a focus on the words in bold print. This will help you complete the table, and will prepare you for the reading.

foundation	reside	persist	inevitable
isolate	perspective	widespread	whereas
civil	couple	decade	tradition
reveal	transform	whereby	intervene
appreciate	factor	fundamental	authority
visible	recover	stable	maintain
occur	coordinate	ideology	reverse
incidence	policy	outcome	contrast

Place each of the vocabulary words under the appropriate heading in the chart below. Use a dictionary if you need help.

Verb	Noun	Adjective	Noun & Verb	Conjunction	Adjective, Noun, & Verb

Bloody Sunday at a Glance...

1   Written and performed by the Irish band U2, "Sunday Bloody Sunday" provides a **revealing perspective** on a tragic event in the modern history of Northern Ireland, the Republic of Ireland, and the United Kingdom. This song was written in 1983, 11 years after 14 **civil** rights protesters, many of whom were teenagers, were killed by the British army on the streets of Derry, Northern Ireland, **whereby** this sad day immediately became known as Bloody Sunday. In order to better **appreciate** this important historical event and the lyrics to this U2 song, it is important to know some **fundamental factors** involved in the recent history of this part of Europe.

2   In the 1920s Ireland was divided by the British government: The Irish Free State and Northern Ireland were formed. Northern Ireland **maintained** its protection under the **authority** of the United Kingdom, **whereas** the Republic of Ireland (as it officially became known as in 1949) formed its own independent nation. This event helped form the **foundation** for the **incidents** of Bloody Sunday. Although Ireland, as it is more commonly known, and Northern Ireland co-existed, many **residents** of Northern Ireland still opposed British rule. This group is commonly known as the Nationalists. However, these **residents** were outnumbered by those in Northern Ireland who wanted to remain under British influence. This group is known as the Unionists. As a result, many Nationalists became increasingly **isolated** and lived with **persistent** hardships under Unionist control. Moreover, there were many militant citizens of Ireland who wanted all of Ireland to be joined as one country. This group formed the Irish Republican Army (IRA). Another point of contention was religion. **Traditionally,** the United Kingdom is Protestant; in **contrast**, the main religion of Ireland is Catholicism. These polarities—the desire for a united Ireland by the Catholic Nationalists and a desire to remain under the British monarchy by the Protestant Unionists, as well as the two opposing religious stances—**coupled** together, led to **decades** of political **instability** and **widespread** social unrest.

3   As the early 1970s arrived, **civil** rights protests in Northern Ireland increased. There was a fear that the Nationalists would defeat the Unionists and that Britain would lose control of Northern Ireland; the **outcome** was **inevitable**. Government **policies** in London determined that the British army **intervene** in Northern Ireland and **coordinate** efforts to try to quell the rising protests from Irish Nationalists. One of these protests, where 14 people were killed, **occurred** on

30 January 1972—Bloody Sunday. The British army **visibly** opened fire on Nationalist protesters as they marched unarmed through the streets of Londonderry. It is this tragic event that U2 sings about in their political protest song, "Sunday Bloody Sunday."

4   Peace treaties and attempts to recover a peaceful co-existence have not yet been successful. Some critics argue that these problems will never disappear and are now **irreversible**. To this day, protests continue, as Ireland and Northern Ireland have yet to **transform** themselves. The two nations remain separated by political and **ideological** differences.

Fill in the table below with three words from this article that are *not* from the AWL, but that are new for you.

Word	Part of Speech	Definition	Sample Sentence

Share your table with a partner.

Reading for Details

The following statements are incorrect. Correct them on the lines below.

1. The 14 civil rights protesters killed were all teenagers.

    _____

2. Presently, the official name of Ireland is the Irish Free State.

    _____

3. The Unionists faced many hardships under the control of the Nationalists.

    _____

4. Northern Ireland is traditionally Catholic, while Ireland is traditionally Protestant.

    _____

5. The Irish Republican Army opened fire on unarmed protesters to try to quell the situation.

    _____

Discuss your answers with a partner. Try to use this chapter's AWL vocabulary as often as you can in your discussion.

Discussion Questions

Discuss the following questions with a partner.

1. What happened to the island of Ireland in the 1920s? Discuss in detail.
2. What were the two main problems that caused so much social unrest in Ireland and Northern Ireland?
3. Why was the British army in Northern Ireland in the early 1970s?
4. What continues to separate Ireland and Northern Ireland these days?

Vocabulary Practice

Definitions

Match the words below with their appropriate definitions.

1. resident 2. outcome 3. fundamental 4. ideology 5. civil 6. whereas 7. authority 8. inevitable	_____ something that you cannot avoid or prevent; so frequent that you always expect it; something that is certain to happen
	_____ the power to give orders to people or the right to do something; the people or an organization who have the power to make decisions or who have a particular area of responsibility; a person with special knowledge
	_____ serious and very important; affecting the most central and important parts of something; forming the necessary basis of something
	_____ a set of beliefs, especially one held by a particular group, that influences the way people behave; a set of ideas on which an economic or political system is based
	_____ a conjunction used to compare or contrast two facts
	_____ the result or effect of an action or event
	_____ a person who lives in a particular place or who has their home there; a doctor working in a hospital who is receiving special advanced training
	_____ connected with the people who live in a country; connected with the state rather than with religion or with the armed forces; involving personal legal matters and not criminal law; polite in a formal way, but possibly not friendly

Definitions taken or adapted from *Oxford Advanced Learner's Dictionary 8th Edition* by A. S. Hornby © Oxford University Press 2010. Reproduced by permission.

Often, as you have seen above, words have multiple meanings. Below is a list of definitions for the word *foundation*. Write a sample sentence that expresses the appropriate meaning for each definition.

a) a layer of bricks, concrete, etc. that forms the solid underground base of a building
b) a principle, an idea, or a fact on which something is based and from which it grows
c) an organization that is established to provide money for a particular purpose, for example for scientific research or charity
d) the act of starting a new institution or organization
e) a skin-coloured cream that is put on the face underneath other makeup

Definitions taken or adapted from *Oxford Advanced Learner's Dictionary 8th Edition* by A. S. Hornby Hornby © Oxford University Press 2010. Reproduced by permission.

Note the coupling of *foundation* with the following adjectives to create phrases that are widely used in English. Use each of them once to write sentences below.

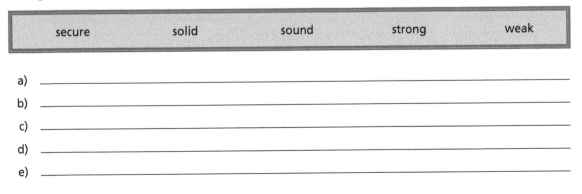

secure	solid	sound	strong	weak

a) _____

b) _____

c) _____

d) _____

e) _____

◎ Expanding Lexical Concepts

Collocations

Use the AWL vocabulary in the text box to form high-frequency collocations with the words below.

visible	recover	policy	persistent
perspective	reverse	widespread	

1. _____ support, corruption, concern, agreement, violence, pollution, suffering
2. analytical, theoretical, visual, contrasting, scientific _____
3. _____ minority, changes, measures, progress, contribution, scar
4. _____ ground, your health, files, data
5. _____ statement, outline; education, government _____
6. _____ attempts, problems, failure, effort, shortages, pain, cough, leak
7. _____ engineering, order, the charge, osmosis, mortgage, discrimination

Using Collocations

Fill in the blanks using the AWL word in parentheses with the correct collocation from the list above.

1. If you get a lot of rest and eat well you should be able to _____ quickly. (recover)
2. The new _____ on education outlines various ways teachers can provide support for students with learning disabilities. (policy)
3. Even though he had taken the prescribed medicine, David still maintained a _____ . (persistent)
4. The newly elected officials enjoyed _____ throughout their term of office. (widespread)
5. Instructors often seat students sequentially or by _____ in elementary school according to their family name. (reverse)
6. Flying at low altitudes in an airplane can offer city engineers an interesting _____ on road and highway design. (perspective)
7. Many of today's computers have built-in mechanisms that allow you to _____ that have been erased by computer viruses. (recover)
8. Even years after surgery, he carried a _____ where the shark had bitten him. (visible)
9. _____ of food rations hampered the progress of rebuilding the war-torn nation. (persistent)
10. Providing yourself with a _____ when confronting a complicated problem may help you resolve the issue sooner. (perspective)

Word Forms

Fill in the blanks with the appropriate form of the AWL vocabulary.

1. After the new _____ the courts decided to release the accused.
   a) reveal   b) revelation   c) revealing   d) revealed

2. The value of goods related to many musicians tends to _____ after they have passed away.

   a) appreciable   b) appreciate   c) appreciation   d) unappreciated

3. _____ that need to be analyzed when making marketing decisions are often related to demographics.

   a) Factor   b) Factoring   c) Factored   d) Factors

4. The Internet provider will be down on Sunday evening to perform routine _____.

   a) maintenance   b) maintaining   c) maintained   d) maintains

5. Many insects go through a wide variety of _____ throughout their life cycle.

   a) transform   b) transformation   c) transforms   d) transformations

6. The degree of severity involving _____ of serious crime is on the rise in many large urban areas.

   a) incidence   b) incidentally   c) incidents   d) incident

7. The lack of _____ in the upper-ranks of the company caused fear amongst investors.

   a) instability   b) unstable   c) stabilization   d) stability

8. Basketball requires a high level of total body _____.

   a) coordinate   b) coordinates   c) coordinator   d) coordination

9. The referees and coaches had to _____ when both the players and fans began to quarrel with each other.

   a) intervention   b) intervenes   c) intervene   d) intervening

10. For decades North Korea has practised a policy of _____.

    a) isolation   b) isolationism   c) isolating   d) isolated

Before Moving On...

About Rock and Roll

It is commonly thought that the birthplace of rock and roll was middle-class America during the 1950s. Rock and roll evolved out of a need to express sex, love, gender, race, and class in a manner that went against the ideology of the times. Stylistically, it grew out of rhythm and blues. One of rock and roll's first icons in the mid-1950s was Elvis Presley. His style appealed to a younger generation, and from his influence emerged other rock-and-roll legends such as the Beatles, the Rolling Stones, Jimi Hendrix, and Nirvana. It is from this long tradition of rock-and-roll musicians that the Irish band U2 emerged.

♫ A Bloody Sunday Song: "Sunday Bloody Sunday"

About the Artist

U2 is a popular Irish rock band from Dublin that formed in the mid-1970s. They have won numerous music awards and still have a huge following today. They released their latest album in 2009 and are most widely recognized by their lead singer Bono, one of the founding members of the ONE campaign—an organization attempting to fight extreme poverty and preventable diseases. You can read more about this organization by researching the ONE campaign on the Internet.

Follow the directions below. You will have two opportunities to hear the song and complete the exercise.

Similar to Chapter 3, this is not a fill-in-the-blanks exercise. Instead, on the right side of the table below you will try to write the main idea(s) expressed in each stanza. The chorus will give you time to think and write, though not much. Again, you are developing the speed at which you organize your thoughts and put them to paper. You're not trying to just copy what the singer says. You are trying to capture the idea that the singer is trying to express. A key word for each stanza is provided as a guiding point for your ideas (note that stanza 5 is asking you to answer a question).

The first one has been done for you. After you listen to the first stanza (the first 50 seconds), study how the example was done, and then begin again.

U2—"Sunday Bloody Sunday"

Keyword	Stanza Summary
Shock ("I can't...")	• unbelievable news reports • can't forget about this tragedy • how long do I have to suffer?
Protest ("Broken...")	
Re-actions to Protest ("But I won't...")	
	Chorus
Family ("And the...")	
	Chorus
What's the metaphor here? ("How long...")	
	Chorus
Pain & Suffering ("Wipe...")	
	Chorus
No Keyword ("And it's...")	

Listen Again!

Listen to the song again and double-check your answers. When you are finished, check your answers with a partner.

Song Survey

In the last column provide a reason for your choice.

1. Were the lyrics easy to understand?	Yes	No	
2. Would you listen to more songs by U2?	Yes	No	
3. Would you recommend this song to your friends?	Yes	No	
4. Is this the kind of song your parents would listen to?	Yes	No	
5. If you were experiencing injustice, would you join a protest?	Yes	No	

Share your answers with a partner.

Song Discussion

Discuss the following questions in small groups.

1. Think about the rhythm and sound of this song. Did you like it? Why or why not? Share your ideas with your group members.
2. Stanza 4 talks about families being torn apart. What is U2 singing about here and why would families be torn apart?

Focus on Speaking

Skills Focus: Summarizing Events Critically

When we report on events of the past, it is often important that we take a critical approach. This allows us to provide a more balanced account of the event(s) in question. Furthermore, by providing as many perspectives as possible, it opens up avenues to where solutions can be found.

Skills in Practice

Think about a problem or conflict from either the past or present in your native country or in another country. When did it occur? Who was involved in the conflict? Was it about one particular incident? What was the fundamental problem? Were there opposing religious or political stances, or a difference in ideologies? Has stability returned to the area? If yes, what was the outcome? If the problem still persists, can you think of any solutions?

Try to provide a balanced, critical summary of the event and try to use as many words from the AWL as possible. Your instructor will give you some time to prepare your thoughts. When you are ready, share your summary of the event with some classmates.

Skills Focus: Thinking on Your Feet

With a partner quickly review the summary you wrote involving the eight tips for being able to think on your feet successfully (Chapter 2, page 33).

Skills in Practice

When you are finished reviewing, prepare to share your ideas again about the conflict you presented in the previous exercise. Remember to keep the AWL vocabulary words from this and other chapters in mind. After your presentation, answer questions from your classmates and your instructor—get ready to think on your feet!

Skills Focus: Listening for Facts and Speech Clarity

Lectures and news reports are often filled with facts and information that can be difficult to hear. This is because speakers surround important points with examples or secondary information that at times can be distracting for listeners. You need to be able to focus your listening and pick out what is important. Furthermore, as you listen, pay close attention to the speaker's pronunciation. Notice its clarity. Even native speakers focus closely on their own pronunciation when the situation requires it. This may include in an important speech or presentation, or as a host of an event, or as in the cases below, as a radio journalist.

Skills in Practice

Exercise A

Tracks 3 and 4: Report on Bloody Sunday Killings and Report on Bloody Sunday Funerals

You will listen to two radio reports from 1972. Each describes a scene related to Bloody Sunday. Listen to the radio reports and fill in the chart below.

Radio Clip 1	
The people involved in the conflict	
The incident or problem being reported	
Location of the report	
Radio Clip 2	
The people involved in the conflict	
The incident or problem being reported	
Location of the report	

Exercise B

Based on the information you have been reading about and listening to in this chapter, prepare a brief 30-second radio report. Skim this chapter's reading again if necessary. Report on the events leading up to Bloody Sunday. Include the following information about the conflict: the people or groups involved, the cause, the location, and any other facts you decide are necessary for the listener to know. When you are finished, prepare to read your radio report to your classmates. Pay special attention to the clarity of your pronunciation (ask your instructor about the pronunciation of words about which you are unsure).

_____

_____

_____

_____

_____

_____

_____

_____

_____

_____

_____

_____

_____

Focus on Reading

Skills Focus: Reading an Exam Question

As you continue with your studies, you will notice that a larger percentage of your grades in any given class will come from writing in-class examinations. Included in these exams will be essays. In order to write an effective in-class essay, you first need to make sure you understand what the question is asking you to do. What exactly does your instructor want from you? Understanding the topic is not enough. You also need to understand *how* your instructor wants you to answer the question—and this information is given to you directly in the question. Below is a list of commonly used directive words in an essay question, or essay prompt. Take a few minutes to look over the list. Then, in a small group discuss *how* an instructor would want you to answer the question. Take some quick notes based on your discussions. (You may want to use a pencil so that you can make changes and/or make additions later.)

Directive	Your Notes
classify	*Into what general category(ies) does this idea belong? Divide cat(s) accordingly.*
compare	
contrast	
critique	
define	
demonstrate	
describe	

discuss	
evaluate	
explain	
identify	
interpret	
justify	
outline	
summarize	
trace	

When you are finished, compare your notes with a partner from a different group (make any changes you think are necessary). After comparing notes with a partner, check your chart against the answer key in the Appendix, page 184.

Thus far in this book you have come across a few essay questions. They include:

A. <u>Demonstrate</u> how Bob Dylan uses four different parts of speech or literary devices to support the theme of humanity's destruction of nature in the song "A Hard Rain's A-Gonna Fall" (Chapter 1, page 17).
B. <u>Discuss</u> the factors involved in the increase of hearing loss of Americans today (Chapter 2, page 36).
C. <u>Describe</u> the benefits of extra-curricular activities for students (Chapter 2, page 38).
D. <u>Critique</u> the following quotation: "Libraries are no longer needed because the Internet has more information that any library does" (Chapter 2, page 38).

 ## Skills in Practice

With a partner discuss *how* you would answer each of the above questions. (What is the instructor expecting you to do?) Be specific with respect to the content of the answer as well.

 ## Focus on Writing

Skills Focus: Writing for an Audience

When you write, it is important that you focus your writing on your audience—the people for whom you are writing. This is influenced by the situation in which you are writing. Different situations will require that you alter your writing style accordingly.

In the exercise below, match the audience with the writing genre that the situation demands.

1. a panel wishing to review the pros and cons of a single global currency
2. a potential employer
3. your English literature professor
4. your friend waiting for you at a restaurant
5. your professor who needs convincing about your ideas
6. a newspaper reader
7. a potential academic program
8. your biology professor
9. your family
10. your creative writing professor
11. your economics professor

a) a science report
b) an email
c) a compare-and-contrast essay
d) a business report
e) an informative article
f) a book report
g) a text message
h) a persuasive essay
i) a cover letter
j) a letter of recommendation
k) a short story

When you're finished check your answers with a partner.

Skills in Practice

Journalism is an excellent example of a profession where knowing your audience is critical. Read the first paragraphs of the following newspaper articles. Write a headline for each.

*Headline:*_____

In this past week the citizens of Rome have not been happy with their leaders. Eighteen members of the local government were charged with bribery, and another seven were found guilty of possessing stolen property, much of it paid for with taxpayer's hard-earned euros. Lawyers representing the state asked for the severest punishments under the law, but Romans will have to wait at least two years before these charges are brought to court. The courts are overwhelmed with other concerns and are painfully behind schedule.

*Headline:*_____

It was five years ago this month that the world experienced its first global-warming refugees. Citizens of the Carteret Atoll, a tiny collection of islands off the coast of Papua New Guinea, were evacuated when rising waters, thought to be the result of melting polar ice caps, started to rise and move inland, covering farmlands and flooding homes. Today, what remains of people's homes is surrounded by algae and tropical fish. The atoll is completely submerged now, and tourism officials are considering turning this once livable town into a scuba diver's paradise, the first of its kind in what could be a growing trend as waters continue to rise around the globe.

Using the following newspaper headlines, write a short introductory paragraph for a newspaper article (study the paragraphs above as examples). Include the following information: time, location, people involved, and the incident or issue the article is about. Before you begin to write, think about who your audience will be.

World leaders sign peace accord

_____
_____
_____
_____
_____
_____

Downtown in ruin after quake

_____

_____

_____

_____

_____

_____

Use the space below to write your own headline and an article about a topic of your choice. Use the AWL vocabulary as frequently as possible.

_____

_____

_____

_____

_____

_____

_____

_____

_____

_____

_____

_____

Additional Vocabulary

Word	Part of Speech	Definition	Sample Sentence

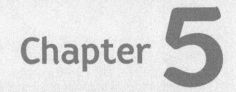

Chapter **5**

Apartheid

Introduction

Study the following three maps. They display the vast area of land controlled by different empires at different points in history. Why might these three empires have wanted to expand to such a large degree? What might have been the advantages or disadvantages? Note, too, the countries they chose to occupy. Why these countries? Why might they have been valuable for that particular empire in that particular time period?

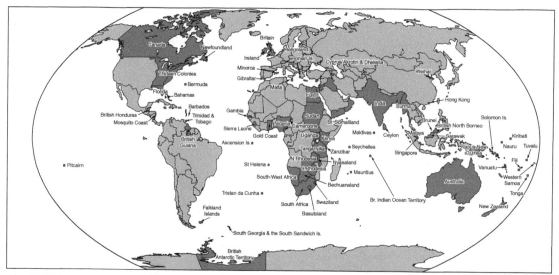

The British Empire or areas that at one time or another were under British control since the mid-sixteenth century

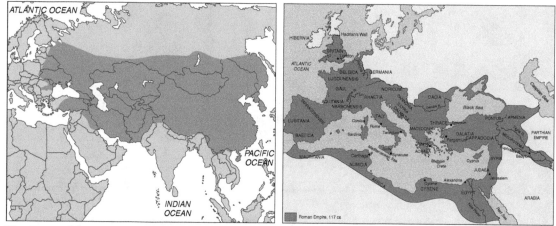

The Mongol Empire, circa 1279

The Roman Empire, circa 117 CE

If your home country were to expand, where do you think it would choose to go? Why? Use the map of the world on page 75 to help you, and explain your choices to a partner.

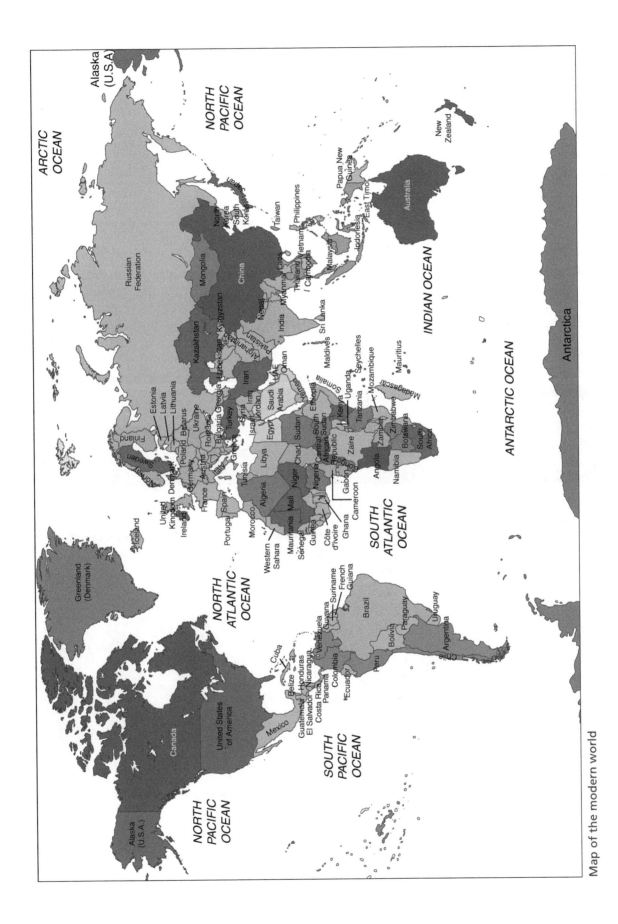

Map of the modern world

Previewing the Reading

Hypothetical situations are often used to make people think about situations that are possible, but that are not likely to occur. Here is a simple example: what would you do if you won a million dollars? Hypothetical questions can create interesting conversations, but they can also serve to help you understand people who have had different life experiences from your own. Preview this chapter's reading by discussing these hypothetical situations with a partner or small group.

Hypothetical questions often begin with the phrase "What would you do if..." or "What if you were...."

What would you do if...

1. ...you were told you could no longer attend the school of your choice?
2. ...you were forced at school to study in a language that was not your own, and in a language you did not want to learn?
3. ...you couldn't marry the person you wanted to?
4. ...you were forced to move away from your home because you were suddenly told you live in the "wrong" neighbourhood?
5. ...you were suddenly not allowed to vote?
6. ...you were not allowed to use certain parts of buildings or public transportation because of your skin colour or nationality?

These are just some examples of situations many black South Africans were placed in during apartheid—the subject of this chapter's reading.

⊘ Apartheid

Academic Word List (AWL) Vocabulary

The following AWL words will appear in this chapter's reading. Before completing the following exercise skim the reading with a focus on the words in bold print. This will help you complete the table, and will prepare you for the reading.

nonetheless	regime	institute	participate
minimize	internal	sustain	legislation
inherently	element	advocate	labour
capable	prohibit	incentive	dramatic
aware	found	convene	hence
enforce	integration	liberal	investment
explicitly	radical	co-operative	minorities
discrimination			

Place each of the above vocabulary words under the appropriate heading in the chart. Use a dictionary if you need help.

Noun	Verb	Adjective	Adverb	Noun & Verb	Noun & Adjective

Apartheid at a Glance...

1   The now-defunct apartheid (an Afrikaans word meaning separateness) system of South Africa presented a fascinating instance of interest-group competition for political advantage. In light of the extreme human-rights abuses stemming from apartheid, it is remarkable that so little attention has been paid to the economic foundations of that torturous social structure. The **conventional** view is that apartheid was devised by affluent whites to suppress poor blacks. In fact, the system sprang from class warfare and was largely the creation of white workers struggling against both the black majority and white capitalists. A haunting union slogan from the 1920s is indicative of the early days of apartheid: "Workers of the world unite, and fight for a white South Africa." White South Africans were setting themselves up to protect their jobs from black Africans happy to work for lower wages. Apartheid was born in the political victory of **radical** white trade unions over both of their rivals.

A Brief History

2   When the British arrived in South Africa in 1796, they quickly conquered the Dutch settlement that had been established in 1652 and set up a government under British law. This **liberal**, individualistic **regime** was **inherently** offensive to the Afrikaners—the Dutch settlers of South Africa—who enjoyed both slavery and a system of law that granted no standing to non-whites. The Boers, as the Afrikaners called themselves, abhorred the British intervention. Following Britain's abolition of South African slavery in 1834, the Afrikaners physically escaped the rule of the British crown in 1835.

3   Moving north, away from Cape Town, the Boers **founded** the Transvaal and the Orange Free State (i.e., free of British domination), and proceeded to establish racist legal **institutions**. The Boers treated brutally, and denied rights to, the relatively few non-whites who resided and worked in their agricultural economy.

4   The Cape Town of nineteenth-century British rule was markedly different. That area experienced some of the most unconstrained racial mixing in the world. A large non-white population, the Cape Coloureds, **participated** in **integrated** schools, churches, businesses, and government institutions. And they voted. A colour-blind franchise was **explicitly** adopted in 1854. As a port city, Cape Town became internationally famous for its laissez-faire social scene. However, when gold was discovered near the Rand River in 1871 (diamonds had been **found** in 1866), the world's richest deposits exerted a powerful magnetic force on the people within the subcontinent.

The Gold Rush

5   The South African gold rush made the natural synergy between white-owned capital and abundant black **labour** overpowering. The gains from **co-operation** between eager British **investors** and

thousands of African workers were sufficient to bridge gaping differences in language and customs. At first, however, the white capitalists dealt directly with only the few English and Afrikaner managers who shared their tongue and work habits. But black workers were becoming **capable** of performing industrial leadership roles in far greater numbers and at far less cost.

6   White workers feared competition from the large supply of cheap African **labour. Hence**, white tradesmen and government officials, including police, regularly harassed African workers. Beginning in the 1890s, the Chamber of Mines, a group of employers, complained regularly of this systematic **discrimination** and attempted to secure better treatment for black workers. Their gesture was neither altruistic nor founded on **liberal** beliefs. Indeed, the mine owners often resorted to racist measures themselves. But here they had a clear economic **incentive: labour** costs were **minimized** where rules were colour-blind. This self-interest was so powerful that it led the chamber to finance the first lawsuits and political campaigns against segregationist **legislation**.

Birth of Apartheid

7   **Nonetheless**, the state instituted an array of legal impediments to the promotion of black workers. The notorious pass laws sought to sharply limit the supply of non-white workers in white employment centres. Blacks were not allowed to become lawful citizens, to live permanently near their work, or to travel without government passports, and were forced into segregated health-care and education systems. Non-whites were also **prohibited** from bringing their families with them while working in the mines (**reinforcing** the transient nature of employment).

8   Together this formed the economic **incentive** that gave birth to apartheid (a system of **legal** racial segregation), a policy **enforced** by the Afrikaner-controlled government from 1948 until 1994.

9   The anti-apartheid movement was a worldwide effort to abolish the South African government's system. For decades, the white **minority** maintained political and economic power by relegating other racial groups to second-class status. From such conditions the anti-apartheid movement sprang into existence both inside and outside South Africa.

The Anti-Apartheid Movement

10   The **internal** anti-apartheid movement took a step forward in 1949, when the conservative African National Congress (ANC) adopted a policy **advocating** resistance in the form of civil disobedience, strikes, and protest marches. In 1959, impatient with the ANC's methods, some members split from the organization to form the more-militant Pan-Africanist Congress (PAC). High on the PAC's list of objectives was the abolition of the cruel law whereby blacks had to carry a pass at all times. It was at one of these anti-pass-law demonstrations, in 1960, that the anti-apartheid movement took a tragic turn with the infamous Sharpeville Massacre, when police opened fire, killing 69 protesters. This event had a **dramatic** influence on the direction of the anti-apartheid movement; the following year, the PAC and the ANC decided to adopt armed resistance against the brutal state.

11   The government declared a state of emergency in the face of the anti-apartheid movement, allowing them to detain people without trial. Both the ANC and PAC were declared "banned" organizations, and some 18,000 demonstrators were arrested, including most of the movement's leadership. As the armed **elements** of the anti-apartheid movement began to follow their policy of sabotage, several ANC leaders were tried for treason at the famous Rivonia Trial in 1964. Eight, including ANC leader Nelson Mandela, were sentenced to life imprisonment. Henceforth, the anti-apartheid movement was largely led from outside South Africa, by ANC members who had escaped into exile.

12   As part of the international anti-apartheid movement, the United Nations imposed sanctions against the South African government. In 1976, the anti-apartheid movement again witnessed public brutality, when, on June 16, police opened fire at a mass rally killing dozens of people.

Ending Apartheid

Nelson Mandela

13 Opposition movements like the National Union of South African Students and the End Conscription Campaign, along with many musicians and several internationally prominent South African writers, played their part in raising **awareness** for the anti-apartheid movement. Demonstrations occurred everywhere. Black neighbourhoods were constantly patrolled by soldiers and police in armoured vehicles; arrests continued by the thousands, and the ANC and PAC retaliated by bombing "soft" targets or unarmed civilians. After years of unrest, the anti-apartheid movement finally prevailed, as the government began to admit the need for change; it could no longer **sustain** the effort required to oppress an overwhelming majority of the population, in the face of constant **internal** chaos, while being internationally and economically ostracized. In 1990, F.W. de Klerk, the new head of the white government, freed Nelson Mandela from prison, and opened negotiations with the anti-apartheid movement. This led, in 1994, to the first truly nationwide multi-racial elections and the inauguration of Nelson Mandela as South Africa's first black president.

Fill in the table below with three words from this article that are *not* from the AWL, but that are new for you.

Word	Part of Speech	Definition	Sample Sentence

Share your table with a partner.

Reading for Details

The following statements are incorrect. Correct them on the lines below.

1. The conventional view is that apartheid was devised by middle-class white workers to suppress the black majority.

   _____

2. The Afrikaners enjoyed slavery under new British law established in 1796.

   _____

3. Cape Town in the 1800s experienced severe forms of segregation.

   _____

4. The pass laws were designed to encourage blacks to search out employment in all white centres.

_____

5. In 1960, the ANC decided to take up arms against the South African government.

_____

Share your answers with a partner. Try to use this chapter's AWL words as often as you can in your discussion.

Discussion Questions

Discuss the following questions with a partner.

1. Summarize the first paragraph together, and then discuss how this first paragraph establishes the author's plan for the first half of this reading. Finally, discuss what this plan is (what will the author write about?).

2. a) In the second paragraph it states that the Boers "abhorred the British intervention." Why might this be the case?

   b) From the sixteenth to the twentieth centuries, many countries came under British control. Why do you think England was so eager to expand at this time in world history? Besides South Africa, can you think of any other countries that came under British control? Other than the influence of language, what other influences might the British have brought to countries they controlled?

3. The reading mentions that the anti-apartheid movement was a "worldwide effort." Why would so many countries around the world care about what is happening in one small country in southern Africa? Why didn't these other countries concern themselves with their own domestic problems?

Vocabulary Practice

Definitions

Match the words below with their appropriate definitions.

1. institute 2. advocate 3. radical 4. regime 5. nonetheless 6. integration 7. legislation 8. incentive	concerning the most basic and important parts of something; thorough and complete; new, different, and likely to have a great effect; a person with very unique and strong opinions
	a law or a set of laws passed by a parliament; the process of making and passing laws
	to support something publicly; a person who supports or speaks in favour of somebody or of a public plan or action
	something that encourages you to do something
	a method or system of government, especially one that has not been elected in a fair way; a method or system of organizing or managing something
	the act or process of combining two or more things so that they work together; the act or process of mixing people who have previously been separated, usually because of colour, race, religion, etc.
	despite this fact
	an organization that has a particular purpose, especially one that is connected with education or a particular profession; the building used by this organization

Definitions taken or adapted from *Oxford Advanced Learner's Dictionary 8th Edition* by A. S. Hornby © Oxford University Press 2010. Reproduced by permission.

Expanding Lexical Concepts

Collocations

Use the AWL vocabulary in the text box to form high-frequency collocations with the words below.

discrimination   labour   minority

dramatic   participate   element

sustain   co-operation

1. basic, critical, crucial, essential, fundamental, important, key, major, necessary, principal, vital, competitive _____

2. manual, physical, forced, hard, cheap, casual, skilled, unskilled, child, migrant, slave, go into, induce _____; _____ market, force

3. be, sound, extremely, highly, very, fairly, quite, rather _____; _____ event

4. large, significant, sizeable, substantial, small, tiny, ethnic, religious, oppressed, persecuted, belong to / discriminate against a / the, government, among a / the _____

5. actively, agree / refuse to, have the opportunity to, be able / allowed / encouraged / invited to _____; _____ in

6. close, full, increased, active, international, local, mutual, economic, military, political, require, ask for, seek, a lack of, a need for _____; in _____ with

7. race / racial, religious, sex / sexual, widespread, blatant, reverse, unlawful, experience, face, suffer, victims of _____; _____ in favour of, on the grounds of

8. be able / unable to, be difficult to, be hard to, be impossible to _____

Using Collocations

Fill in the blanks using the AWL word in parentheses with the correct collocation from the list above. More than one answer may be suitable at times.

1. The convention organizers were _____ in the questions and answer session at the end of the day. (participate)

2. The present levels of fresh-water consumption will _____ in the near future. (sustain)

3. A thesis statement is an _____ of any well-written essay. (element)

4. The police will _____ from the public regarding the _____ leading up to the mayor's death. (co-operation / dramatic)

5. When an _____ is oppressed, they will inherently stick together. (minority)

6. _____ have the option of seeking legal aid in many countries. (discrimination)

7. Expectant mothers often _____ unexpectedly. (labour)

Word Forms

Fill in the blanks with the appropriate form of the AWL vocabulary.

1. The committee will _____ at 5:00 PM on Wednesday.
   a) convention   b) convene   c) convenes   d) conventional

2. The company _____ will be commemorated after dinner, but before the slide show.
   a) founded   b) found   c) founder   d) unfounded

3. _____ bleeding is a serious condition that requires immediate medical attention.
   a) Internally   b) Internalize   c) Internalizing   d) Internal

4. Law-_____ officers often have to deal with precarious situations.
   a) enforcing   b) enforcement   c) enforces   d) enforced

5. Wartime _____ are depicted as heroes in many Hollywood films.
   a) liberate   b) liberalism   c) liberator   d) liberators

6. A sound _____ at an early age can provide financial security for your future.
   a) invest   b) investing   c) investment   d) reinvesting

7. _____ learning has the potential to increase one's ability to socialize in both large and small groups.
   a) Co-operative   b) Co-operatively c) Co-operation   d) Co-operated

8. A fundamental element for the continued success of humanity will be our ability to create a _____ environment in which to live.
   a) sustainable   b) sustenance   c) unsustainable   d) sustaining

9. _____ often receive complaints from the public if they fail to meet the demands of the common people.
   a) Legislators   b) Legislate   c) Legislated   d) Legislator

10. A _____ democracy functions best when access to information is granted to any individual who seeks it.
    a) participation   b) participant   c) participatory   d) participating

Before Moving On...
About... Your Choice!

The song you are going to listen to for this chapter is once again from the folk music genre (specifically African Folk). It is a testament to the power and popularity of the lyrics typical of folk music. There are, however, numerous musical genres that contain songs that deal with apartheid. Do some research on a musical genre of your choice. Be sure to avoid doing research on those genres already dealt with in Chapters 1–4. You do not have to actually find a song that deals with apartheid; instead, focus your attention on a style of music that you enjoy listening to. Take some notes on this genre and prepare an informal presentation for a classmate. You may use the descriptions of genres in the previous chapters as a guide. Record your notes in point form below, instead of writing sentences. This will help you focus on speaking instead of writing.

_____

_____

_____

_____

_____

♪ An Apartheid Song: "Weeping"

About the Artist

Vusi Mahlasela, better known as "The Voice" in his home of South Africa, is an African folk musician well known for songs that connect echoes of a cruel apartheid era with hope for a brighter future. As a child, Mahlasela taught himself how to play guitar, and slowly rose to international fame, touring globally and playing at the FIFA 2010 World Cup Kick-off Concert in South Africa. He also works as an official ambassador of Nelson Mandela's HIV/AIDS initiative. Mahlasela is also an active supporter of the ONE campaign, which you read about earlier in Chapter 4's discussion of U2. The song "Weeping" is itself in reference to apartheid, and is a cover of a song written by Dan Heymann, a white South African soldier forced by his government into defending the apartheid policy.

Listen to the song and try to fill in the blanks. You will have two opportunities to hear the song.

Vusi Mahlasela—"Weeping"

I knew a man who lived in fear.
It was huge, it was angry, it was drawing near.
_____ _____ _____, a secret place
was the shadow of the demon he could never face.
He built a wall of steel and flame   5
And men with guns _____ _____ _____ _____.
Then standing back he made it plain
that the _____ would never ever rise again.
But the fear and the fire and the guns remained.

It doesn't matter now. It's over anyhow.   10
_____ _____ _____ _____ _____ _____ _____ _____.
But as the night came round I heard _____ _____ _____.
It wasn't roaring, it was weeping.
It wasn't roaring, it was weeping.

And then one day the neighbours came.   15
They were _____ to know about the smoke and flame.
They stood around outside the wall,
but of course there was nothing to be heard at all.
"_____ _____," he said, "We've reached our goal,
the threat is under firm control.   20
As long as peace and order _____,
I'll be damned if I can see a reason to explain,
why the fear and the fire and the guns remained."

It doesn't matter now. It's over anyhow.
_____ _____ _____ _____ _____ _____ _____.   25
But as the night came round I heard _____ _____ _____.
It wasn't roaring, it was weeping.
It wasn't roaring, it was weeping.

Say over, say over, say over
And say over, say over, say over (x3).   30

It doesn't matter now. It's over anyhow.

_____ _____ _____ _____ _____ _____.   35

But as the night came round I heard _____ _____ _____.
It wasn't roaring, it was weeping (x9).

Listen Again!

Listen to the song again and double-check your answers. When you are finished, check your answers with a partner.

Song Survey

In the last column, provide a reason for your choice.

1. Were the lyrics easy to understand?	Yes	No	
2. Would you listen to more songs by Vusi Mahlasela?	Yes	No	
3. Is this the kind of song your parents would listen to?	Yes	No	
4. Now that you know the background story to this song, would you recommend it to your friends?	Yes	No	
5. Would you consider this a political protest song?	Yes	No	

Share your answers with a partner.

Song Discussion

Discuss the following questions in small groups.

1. Reread lines 1 and 2. What is the "fear" that the man constantly lived with? And why would this cause so much fear?
2. Reread lines 13 and 14. What is the "it" referred to here? And why is this "it" weeping?
3. There are at least two examples of personification in this song. Explain how the personification works in each instance, and then discuss the effect these images may have on the listener.
4. The songwriter was a white South African who was forced to join the military and help defend the apartheid regime. What would you have done in this situation? How would you feel about being forced to defend something you didn't believe in?

Focus on Reading

Skills Focus: Paraphrasing and Quoting

In Chapter 2, you learned how to summarize a reading (see pages 32–33 to review). In this chapter, you will learn how to paraphrase and quote material, and then how to combine the three (summarizing, paraphrasing, and quoting) whenever necessary.

Understanding the Differences

Summary	Rewrite the main idea(s) in your own words. It is usually much shorter than the original (and even much shorter than a paraphrase [see below]) and focuses only on one central point (or the main point and its supporting details, if the source material is lengthy). The author of the original must be cited as well.
Paraphrase	Rewrite the source material in your own words. It is usually shorter than the original and only focuses on a few key points. The author of the original must be cited as well.
Quotation	It is identical to the source material, but only uses a small portion of the original. The passage being used must be exactly, word for word, as it is in the original, and it is usually in quotation marks. The author of the original must be cited as well.

The differences between the three of these can seem subtle, especially between a paraphrase and a summary. With a partner review the differences above. Take a few minutes to discuss these differences in detail.

Skills in Practice

Imagine that you are writing a literature paper on hope and the twentieth-century novel. In your research, you come across the following passage from George Orwell's novel *1984*. You find that it is perfect for your paper. Read the passage and then complete the exercise below:

> That was all, and he was already uncertain whether it had happened. Such incidents never had any sequel. All that they did was to keep alive in him the belief, or hope, that others besides himself were the enemies of the Party.
>
> *[Source: George Orwell, 1984, Signet Classic (CITY: Penguin, 1950) 18].*

You could use this short passage in your essay in one of three ways: as a summary, paraphrase, or quotation. Label each sentence below as a summary, paraphrase, or quotation.

_____ The unnamed event only managed "to keep alive in him the belief, or hope" that others existed too that the Party disliked (Orwell, *1984*).

_____ The point of this short passage is to demonstrate that hope, in situations of great stress, can help maintain one's sanity (Orwell, *1984*).

_____ An unnamed event occurred, which made the protagonist question the event's existence. Although he was sure that these kinds of things do not recur, the event produced in him a hope that others also existed of whom the Party was not fond (Orwell, *1984*).

There are numerous reasons why you might want to summarize, paraphrase, or quote in your writing. Add two reasons to the list below, then share them with a partner.

- to add support, or provide an example for a point you are arguing for
- to call extra attention to a credible passage that defends your point by quoting it directly
- to introduce a counter-argument
- to reference other work that is similar to yours
- _____
- _____

Tips that will help you master this skill:

1. Reread the text you are working on and focus on the main ideas.
2. Decide what the main idea of the text is, and summarize it in your own words.
3. Note points in the text that support the main idea, and paraphrase them.
4. Watch for material that you could quote directly (passages that are clear and clearly support your own point).

Focus on Writing

Skills Focus: How to Quote Source (or Secondary) Material

Deciding what material to quote in your paper can sometimes be tricky, but with practice you will get better. Fortunately, learning *how* to quote material is not very difficult. If you follow these few simple guidelines, you should be fine. For more complicated matters, however, you may want to seek out a style guide (American Psychological Association [APA], Chicago Manual of Style [CMOS], Modern Language Association [MLA], etc.) that is specific to the course you are studying, or ask your instructor for more specific guidance.

Generally, we use quotation marks when we want to quote something directly (word for word) from a source material. There are three popular ways to do this. Every manner requires that the sentence with the quotation in it be grammatically sound.

For shorter material (as a general rule, for material less than four lines) there are two styles you can use to quote:

I. Incorporate the quoted material inside the body of your sentence.
   ✓ 1. Orwell writes that "he was already uncertain" about the situation he was in (Orwell, *1984*).
   ✗ 2. The protagonist was confused, "he was already certain."
   ✗ 3. Although he was already uncertain, he knew it could never happen again (Orwell, *1984*).
   ✓ 4. Due to his fear, "he was already uncertain" regarding his position (Orwell, *1984*).
      – The second sentence is not grammatically sound (a comma has been used to join two sentences [a comma splice]). Also, the quotation is copied incorrectly ("*un*certain" not "certain"), and the material isn't cited (Orwell, *1984*).
      – The third sentence fails to use quotation marks.
      – Notice how sentences 1 and 4 are still grammatically sound (you could remove the quotation marks and still have a well-written sentence).

II. Introduce the quoted material using a colon (:), while maintaining a grammatically sound sentence.
   ✓ 1. Orwell indicates the protagonist's feelings regarding the situation he was in: "he was already uncertain" (Orwell, *1984*).
   ✗ 2. It is obvious that the protagonist is confused: "he was already uncertain," which tells the readers his feelings (Orwell, *1984*).
   ✗ 3. "He was already uncertain": he knew it could never happen again.
   ✓ 4. His fear clearly demonstrated his feelings about his position: "he was already uncertain" (Orwell, *1984*).
      – The second sentence adds a comma and then extra information. After a quotation that is introduced with a colon (:) you should end the sentence immediately after the reference (see sentence 1). Add any extra information in the following sentence.
      – In sentence three, a colon (:) is not used to introduce a quotation (as a general rule, never begin a sentence with a quotation mark). The colon (:) must come before the quotation mark. The source material isn't cited either (Orwell, *1984*).
      – Again, sentences 1 and 4 are grammatically sound.

There are two punctuation rules regarding I and II to keep in mind as well:

a)   *periods* and *commas* should be kept *inside* the quotation marks

> Orwell indicates that "he was already uncertain,✍" but that these events "never had any sequel.✍"

The only exception to this rule is if the material is being cited. In such cases the period follows the citation.

> Orwell indicates that "he was already uncertain," but that these events "never had any sequel" (Orwell 18).✍

b)   place all *other punctuation marks outside* the quotation mark.

> Can the reader really tell if "he was already uncertain"?✍

For longer material, or a block quotation (four or more lines—but again, consult a style guide as different disciplines have slightly different requirements), follow these guidelines:

- Introduce the block quotation with a colon (:).
- Indent the block quotation five spaces (similar to a new paragraph).
- Do not use any quotation marks.
- Double or single space according to your style guide.
- Cite the source in parentheses after the final period (again, check your style guide).
- After the block quotation, return to using regular spacing and paragraph margins (usually explaining the quotation in your own words).

While working with quotations, keep in mind the following:

1.   It is important that you do not overuse block quotations. It will interrupt the flow of your writing. (As a rough rule, estimate about one block quotation for every three pages of a double-spaced essay.)
2.   Avoid ending a paragraph with a quotation. After each quotation you should explain its significance to your paper.
3.   The following reporting verbs (verbs that indicate what someone else has said or written) will help add variety to your writing (use them).

> For example: In his novel *1984*, Orwell... adds, announces, argues, comments, complains, criticizes, declares, estimates, exclaims, notes, observes, points out, predicts, proclaims, proposes, remarks, replies, responds, states, suggests, thinks, writes....

4.   Using quotations will help strengthen your argument, and they will add some variety to your writing. Don't be afraid to quote when necessary—just don't overdo it. You still have other forms of evidence you can use to defend your ideas (data, statistics, and summaries). Keep in mind, too, that the majority of your essays should still be written in your own words.

◎ Skills in Practice

Use the skills you have learned in the Focus on Reading and Focus on Writing sections to write a paper about the education system in South Africa during apartheid. You will need to summarize, paraphrase, and quote source material in this paper. Also, you should review the skills you learned in Chapter 3 about evaluating sources of information—this will prove helpful in your research. Here is the essay question, then: *Discuss how the South African government used the national education system to promote the ideals of apartheid.*

🎧 Focus on Listening

Skills Focus: Listening for Gist and Details

Take a minute to study the table below. What is different about the information provided in each example on the right side of the table?

Table A

	Example A
Gist—Listening *to*...	weather forecast for Toronto, ON, Thursday June 12
Details—Listening *for*...	am—cloudy with rain, 15° pm—clearing up, 23°
	Example B
Gist—Listening *to*...	Disney business plan in July next year to increase stock value
Details—Listening *for*...	increase sales 5% reduce expenditures 3% restructure managerial staff

Listening for Gist

Track 5: Imperialism in Africa

Listening for gist requires that you be able to identify the main ideas being presented to you in any listening activity: a scene in a movie, a radio program, a lecture by a professor, or even in a speech (as you will hear in Chapter 9). Understanding gist requires that you listen for the overall theme or main ideas being presented.

imperialism—a system whereby one country takes control of another country or area, often by military force

South Africa was by no means the only African nation to suffer under imperialism. Imperialism has played a significant role in the shaping of political boundaries for thousands of years, with European countries dominating this trend over the last few centuries. You are going to listen to the beginning of a lecture on European imperialism in Africa. This excerpt is of a professor reviewing the key points of a previous lecture he gave. In the first exercise, you should only concentrate on understanding the gist of the piece. Before you begin, study the map for extra reference. How many countries were independent in 1914? Do you know the names of these countries? List them here:

_____

_____

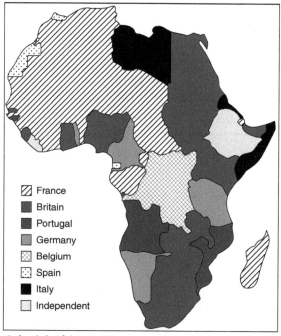

France
Britain
Portugal
Germany
Belgium
Spain
Italy
Independent

Colonial Africa, 1914

Skills in Practice

Five of the eight main ideas presented in the listening piece are listed below, out of order. As you listen the first time, place them in the correct sequential order. When you listen again, focus on the three main ideas discussed in the talk, which are not listed below. What phrase could you use to describe them? List them in the space provided.

1 _____

____ Missionaries

____ Industrial Revolution

____ Speed and Goal of Colonization

____ Joseph Conrad

6 _____

____ European Perspective

8 _____

When you are finished check your answers with a partner.

Listening for Details

Listening for details requires that you do exactly that—listen for more specific details. This is essential for obtaining small points of important information to which a speaker may refer. This skill requires that you listen *for* something specific (see Table A on the previous page for an example).

Skills Focus Review: Lecture Note-taking Skills

What do you remember from Chapter 2 about note-taking skills? Take a minute to think about this. What were some of the key points about note-taking that were discussed? Share what you can recall with a partner. When you are finished your discussion, return to pages 34–36 to review this skill.

Skills in Practice

Listen to the talk on colonialism in Africa again, and combine your note-taking skills (Chapter 2, pages 34–36) with listening for details. Together these should help you capture the more important details of the piece. Use the eight sub-headings from Exercise A as an outline to guide your notes.

Focus on Speaking

◎ Skills Focus: Defending a Point of View

Conflict Resolution—Thinking Outside the Box

Thinking outside the box is an idiom that means to think in a way that provides a new perspective on any situation. It creates new ways to find solutions and is an excellent skill to have for problem solving.

1. Below is a list of conflicts. They begin with simple problems, but increase in difficulty and complexity. Take a moment now to read each of the conflicts, and then complete the first box in row (h).

2. Your goal is to think outside the box and create new ideas that may help resolve these conflicts. This is an important first step in conflict resolution. Furthermore, solving conflicts often involves discussing them with others, so work together with a small group to complete the chart below (note that there is only room for two ideas in column 3, so choose your solutions carefully). Remember to use words from the AWL whenever possible in your discussion.

Conflict	Simple Solutions	Solutions Outside The Box
Example: 2 children; 1 cookie	• share the cookie (1/2 each)	• *bake more cookies* • *give the cookie away*
a) 3 bicycles; 4 people	• take turns riding and walking	• •
b) daily traffic jams in big cities that create intense pollution and hours wasted in cars	• bus-only lanes to improve traffic and encourage public transportation	• •
c) pregnancy (woman wants to keep the baby; man doesn't want to keep the baby)	• couple separates; man pays monthly fees to help support child (child support)	• •
d) shortage of fresh water in Australia	• increase water tax so people are more cautious about water usage	• •
e) nuclear weapons in Iran and North Korea	• financial rewards if countries stop producing nuclear weapons	• •
f) the problem in Ireland and Northern Ireland discussed in Chapter 4 (it is still not resolved)	• no easy solution here; you will have to think outside the box	• •
g) 1970 apartheid in South Africa (how would you have tried to solve the problem?)	•	• •
h) Add a conflict from your own experiences here	•	• •

Skills in Practice

Imagine that your classroom is an office for an organization that helps countries resolve conflicts (many such organizations exist in the world today). Your organization has been put in charge of providing suggestions and solutions for problems (b), (d), and (f) in the chart on page 90. However, only one possible solution will be accepted for each problem. Find a partner from another group and narrow down your solutions to one per problem. As in any workplace, the person whose idea is selected is often rewarded. Ensure that as many of your ideas as possible are on the final list. You will have to argue and defend your ideas, proving their superiority over other ideas. Here are some tips for your success:

1. Identify the strongest points for each of your ideas.
2. Provide reasons or evidence for each of these points.
3. Listen carefully to your opponent's ideas and reasons for supporting them, and identify the weakest points in your opponent's ideas.
4. Provide reasons or evidence for why their idea(s) is weak.
5. Conclude by restating the most important point(s) of your idea.

Additional Vocabulary

Word	Part of Speech	Definition	Sample Sentence

Chapter 6

Race Relations in America

Introduction

 Thus far you have been exposed to various types of music genres: folk, beat, rock, and a genre of your choice. Identify three or four more genres of music that have not yet been dealt with, and prepare to perform a class survey. The purpose of the survey is twofold: one, to get a feel for what your classmates think of the music you have listened to in the first half of the book; and two, to uncover the overall musical preferences and habits of your classmates. Work in small groups to create five or six questions that you could ask in your survey. When your survey is complete, look for trends or patterns in the responses. With this data you should be able to make some conclusions about the musical preferences and habits of your classmates. Discuss the conclusions with your group. When you are finished find a partner from another group and share your results.

Previewing the Reading

Track 6: Art and Hip Hop

Preview the upcoming reading by listening to a short commentary on art and hip-hop music by Jiro Kohl, a former associate editor at *Mass Appeal* magazine. Take notes and summarize his comments. Then, with a partner, discuss his ideas. What are some interesting points he makes? Do you agree with him? Why or why not? Try to elaborate on his comments.

Race Relations in America

Academic Word List (AWL) Vocabulary

The following AWL words will appear in this chapter's reading. Before completing the exercise below skim the reading with a focus on the words in bold print. This will help you complete the table below, and will prepare you for the reading.

aspect	contemporary	culture	illegal
global	sexually	contribute	negative
community	focus	complex	clarity
feature	irrational	context	resource
margin	involve	shift	achieve
convince	attitude	theme	style
ethnic	commit	diverse	item
precise	consequence	equate	
predominantly	interact		

Place each of the above vocabulary words under the appropriate heading in the chart. Use a dictionary if you need help.

Noun	Verb	Noun & Verb	Noun & Adjective	Adjective	Adverb	Noun, Adjective, & Verb

Race Relations in America at a Glance...

1   For many music critics, the 1990 release of Public Enemy's album *Fear of a Black Planet* provided the launching pad for the future successes of rap and hip hop in the mainstream **global culture**.

2   Rap music is a confusing and noisy element of **contemporary** American popular **culture** that continues to draw a great deal of attention to itself. On the one hand, music and **cultural** critics praise rap's role as an educational tool, pointing out that black female rappers are a rare example of aggressive pro-women lyricists in popular music, and defend rap's ghetto stories as real-life reflections that should draw attention to the burning problems of racism and economic oppression, rather than to questions of obscenity. On the other hand, news-media attention on rap seems fixated on instances of violence at rap concerts, rap producers' **illegal** use of music samples, gangster rap's lurid fantasies of cop killing, and black-nationalist rappers' suggestions that white people are the devil's disciples. These celebratory and inflammatory aspects in rap and the media coverage of them bring to the fore several long-standing debates about popular music and **culture**. Some of the more contentious disputes revolve around the following questions: Can violent images incite violent action, can music set the state for political mobilization, do **sexually** explicit lyrics **contribute** to the so-called moral breakdown of society, and finally, is this really music anyway?

3   If these debates about rap music are not confusing enough, rappers also engage them in contradictory ways. Some defend the work of gangster rappers and at the same time consider it a **negative** influence on black youths. Rappers who criticize America for its perpetuation of racial and economic discrimination also share conservative ideas about personal responsibility, and call for self-improvement strategies in the black **community** that **focus** heavily on personal behaviour as the cause and solution for crime, drugs, and **community** instability.

4   Rap music brings together a tangle of some of the most **complex** social, **cultural**, and political issues in **contemporary** American society. Rap's contradictory articulations are not signs of absent intellectual **clarity**; they are a common **feature** of **community** and popular-**cultural** dialogues that always offer more than one **cultural**, social, or political viewpoint. These unusually abundant multifaceted conversations seem **irrational** when they are severed from the social **contexts** where everyday struggles over **resources**, pleasure, and meanings take place.

5   Rap music is a black **cultural** expression that prioritizes black voices from the **margins** of urban America. From the outset, in the mid-1970s, rap music has articulated the pleasures and problems of black urban life in **contemporary** America. Rappers speak with the voice of personal experience, taking on the identity of the observer or narrator. Male rappers often speak from the perspective of a young man who wants social status in a locally meaningful way. Female

rappers sometimes tell stories from the perspective of a young woman who is skeptical of male protestations of love or a girl who has been **involved** with a drug dealer and cannot sever herself from his dangerous **lifestyle**. Some raps speak to the failures of black men to provide security and attack men where their manhood seems most vulnerable: their wallet. Some tales are of one sister telling another to leave an abusive lover.

6   Like all **contemporary** voices, the rapper's voice is imbedded in powerful and dominant technological, industrial, and ideological institutions. Rap tales are told in elaborate and ever-changing black slang and refer to black **cultural** figures and rituals, mainstream film, video and television characters, and little-known black heroes. For rap's language wizards, all images, sounds, ideas, and icons are ripe for **recontextualization**, pun, mockery, and celebration.

7   Rap's stories continue to articulate the **shifting** terms of black **marginality** in **contemporary** American **culture**. Even as rappers **achieve** what appears to be central status in commercial **culture**, they are far more vulnerable to censorship efforts than highly visible white rock artists. Even as they struggle with the tension between fame and rap's gravitational pull toward local urban narratives, for the most part, rappers continue to craft stories that represent the creative fantasies, perspectives, and experiences of racial **marginality** in America.

8   Rap went relatively unnoticed by mainstream music and popular **culture** industries until independent music entrepreneur Sylvia Robinson released "Rapper's Delight," by the Sugar Hill Gang in 1979.

9   For more than a decade, rap music survived several death knells, Hollywood mockery, and radio bans; indeed, new artists continued to emerge from the hip-hop scene. Between 1987 and 1990, a number of critical music and industry changes took place. Public Enemy became rap's first superstar group with the release of *Fear of a Black Planet*, and media attention to its black-nationalist stance intensified.

10   By 1989, MTV started playing rap music videos on a relatively regular basis, **convincing** music-industry executives that rap music, despite its "blackness" in **attitude**, **style**, speech, music, and **themes**, was a substantial success with white teenagers.

11   Rap's **cultural** address and its **focus** on **marginal** identities may appear to be in opposition to its crossover appeal for people from different racial or **ethnic** groups and social positions. How can this black public dialogue speak to the thousands of white suburban youth who are critical to the record-sales successes of many of rap's more prominent stars? How can one argue that rap is **committed culturally** and emotionally to the pulse, pleasures, and problems of black urban life in the face of such **diverse** constituencies?

12   To suggest that rap is a black **item** that prioritizes black **culture** and articulates the problems of black urban life does not deny the pleasure and participation of others. In fact, numerous genres of black music before rap (e.g., blues, jazz, rhythm and blues, and early rock and roll) became popular **precisely** because of extensive white participation. **Consequently**, the fact that many white teenagers have become rap fans is consistent with the history of black music in America and should not be **equated** with a **shift** in rap's **focus** away from black fans. Black **culture** in the United States has always had "bi-focal" elements, speaking to a black audience in a larger **predominantly** white **context**. Rap music shares this history of **interaction** with many previous black oral and music traditions.

13   The song "Fear of a Black Planet" (from the album of the same name) is representative of this bi-focal element. Its lyrics deal with some of the anxieties and frustrations of black Americans in the late 1980s and early 1990s, and it was also one of the first albums to be fully embraced by white teenagers across the United States. Many critics cite "Fear of a Black Planet" as largely responsible for propelling rap and hip hop into the mainstream.

Fill in the table below with three words from this article that are *not* from the AWL, but that are new for you.

Word	Part of Speech	Definition	Sample Sentence

Share your table with a partner.

Reading for Details

Each of the following statements is incorrect. Correct them on the lines below.

1. Rap music is no longer as popular today it was in the 1990s.

   _____

2. The contradictions apparent in rap-music lyrics are a sign that songwriters lack intellectual clarity.

   _____

3. Rap music is consistently produced using the same style of slang.

   _____

4. Rap was considered popular and mainstream in 1979 when "Rapper's Delight" was recorded.

   _____

5. It was rare in 1990 that the white community (here white teenagers) enjoyed music produced by the black community.

   _____

Share your answers with a partner. Try to use this chapter's AWL vocabulary as often as you can.

Discussion Questions

◉ Discuss the following questions with a partner.

1. In paragraph 2, the author of the article notes how the news media concentrates on the negative aspects of rap instead of its positive influences. Why do you think this is the case?
2. At the end of paragraph 2, the author introduces some important questions regarding rap and the media. Discuss some of them, as follows: Can violent images incite violent action? Can music influence political action? Do lyrics heavy with sexual imagery corrupt society?
3. "The biggest missing aspect of hip hop is...the selling of the art form instead of the selling of the product." Chuck D, one of the members of Public Enemy, said this in a 2010 interview, 20 years after the release of *Fear of a Black Planet*. First, discuss what he means by this. Second, what can you infer about his attitude toward modern-day hip hop?

Vocabulary Practice

Definitions

Match the words below with their appropriate definitions.

1. ethnic 2. interact 3. precise 4. contemporary 5. focus 6. aspect 7. context 8. equate	_____ to give attention, effort, etc. to one particular subject, situation, or person rather than another; to adjust something so that you can see things clearly; the thing or person in which people are most interested
	_____ to think that something is the same as something else or is as important
	_____ the situation in which something happens and that helps you to understand it; the words that come just before and after a word, phrase, or statement and help you to understand its meaning
	_____ connected with or belonging to a nation, race, or people that shares a cultural tradition
	_____ clear and accurate; used to emphasize that something happens at a particular time or in a particular way
	_____ belonging to the same or present time; a person who lives or lived at the same time as somebody else, especially somebody who is about the same age
	_____ a particular part or feature of a situation, an idea, a problem, etc.; a way in which it may be considered
	_____ to communicate with somebody, especially while you work, play or spend time with them

Definitions taken or adapted from *Oxford Advanced Learner's Dictionary 8th Edition* by A. S. Hornby © Oxford University Press 2010. Reproduced by permission.

Check a learner's dictionary for usages of the word *margin*. Note its multiple uses. The *Oxford Advanced Learner's Dictionary* lists seven different usages for *margin*. In the spaces below, list five usages. Provide a brief explanation for each usage and a model sentence.

1. _____
   _____

2. _____
   _____

3. _____
   _____

4. _____
   _____

5. _____
   _____

Expanding Lexical Concepts

Collocations

Use the AWL vocabulary in the text box to form high-frequency collocations with the words below.

complex	community	feature
theme	shift	irrational
resource	consequence	
attitude	item	

1. favourable, friendly, positive, sympathetic, aggressive, bad, hostile, negative, carefree, laid-back, liberal, conservative, rigid, a change in / of _____; _____ problem, toward

2. large, small, close-knit, tight-knit, thriving, vibrant, local, immigrant, religious, Asian, black, Christian, Muslim, farming, rural, academic, business, gay, scientific _____; _____ centre, college, service, work

3. appear, be, seem, become, consider sth, regard sth as, seemingly _____; _____ behaviour, judgment

4. a) sound, enormously, extremely, highly, particularly, increasingly, relatively _____

   b) vast, entertainment, housing, industrial, office, shopping, inferiority, guilty _____

   (Note the difference in pronunciation between the two answers here.)

5. individual, particular, specific, essential, important, expensive, luxury, collector's, news _____

6. basic, essential, distinct, distinguishing, dominant, notable, prominent, striking, endearing, interesting, common, permanent, built-in, additional, handsome, rugged _____

7. important, vital, sufficient, limited, finite, scarce, renewable, non-renewable, additional, invaluable, untapped, natural, human, learning, library _____; _____ centre, management, constraints

8. dramatic, fundamental, profound, radical, substantial, slight, gradual, sudden, irreversible, work, double, split, day, early, night, afternoon, evening, morning, weekend _____; _____ away from, occurs, takes place

9. basic, central, dominant, underlying, universal, familiar, recurring, related, unifying, contemporary, historical, religious, campaign, develop / discuss / examine / explore a _____; _____ song, park

10. far-reaching, profound, adverse, catastrophic, fatal, serious, unfortunate, direct, indirect, long-term, short-term, environmental, as a _____

Using Collocations

Fill in the blanks using the AWL word in parentheses with the correct collocation from the list above. More than one answer may be suitable at times.

1. Criminals who commit a minor offence are often sentenced to _____. (community)

2. Wind energy is one type of _____. (resource)

3. The athlete's village at the most recent Olympics was to be turned into a _____ for low-income families after the Games. (complex)

4. Even with proper parenting, children can still develop severe _____. (attitude)

5. Fifty years ago, a colour TV was considered a _____. (item)
6. The _____ of the last election was predominantly conservative. (theme)
7. Her successes in life are _____ of her hard work. (consequence)
8. Current trends in energy consumption indicate a _____ oil and gas toward sustainable alternatives. (shift)
9. An _____ of infants are their ability to make even hardened individuals smile. (feature)
10. _____ is often difficult to predict. (behaviour)

Word Forms

Fill in the blanks with the appropriate form of the AWL vocabulary.

1. Solutions to complex _____ problems such as climate change require high levels of collaboration between all nations.
   a) globalization   b) globally   c) global   d) globe

2. If you are confused about something, you should ask for _____.
   a) clarifying   b) clarification   c) clarity   d) clarify

3. Cities such as Toronto have an extremely high level of ethnic _____.
   a) diversify   b) diversifying   c) diversification   d) diversity

4. Despite his efforts, Dave's mom remained _____ about his whereabouts yesterday evening.
   a) convinced   b) unconvinced   c) convincing   d) convinces

5. Despite numerous families moving out of the neighbourhood, it remained a _____ influential area to live in.
   a) predominating   b) predominantly   c) predominate   d) predominance

6. Uneducated people are often inaccurately portrayed as _____ in the mainstream media.
   a) uncultured   b) cultured   c) culturally   d) culture

7. Despite his newfound misgivings, he had already _____ to the project.
   a) commitment   b)commitments   c) committed   d) committing

8. Although she had regretted her comments, she was unable to _____ the short-term consequences they had.
   a) negative   b) negatively   c) negate   d) negating

9. The total _____ collected exceeded the organization's goal.
   a) contribute   b) contributor   c) contributes   d) contributions

10. _____ such as those described in her book are deserving of praise.
    a) Achievements   b) Achievement   c) Achievable   d) Achieving

Before Moving On...

About Hip Hop

Hip hop is often described as a popular element of American culture, with integrated elements of rap, sampling, scratching, and "beat-boxing" producing its distinct sound. Rapping (the vocal, lyrical element of hip hop) has its origin in the 1970s, in black inner-city America. The South Bronx, a borough of New York City, is cited as the modern birthplace of hip hop, but

KRS-One

music historians argue that it can be traced back to African roots. Spoken-word poets like Gil Scott-Heron, who spoke about histories accompanied by music, were also responsible for the birth of modern rap and hip hop. Other modern influences included Jamaican dub (brought to New York by the large Jamaican immigrant community), and 1970s disco (hip hop being a reaction against it). Hip hop grew through the 1980s and finally began to gain commercial success in the 1990s with groups like Public Enemy and A Tribe Called Quest. Today hip-hop culture continues to inspire and motivate musicians and their followers around the world. Its immense influence has moved well beyond just the music industry. In the words of one of hip hop's pioneers, KRS-One, "Hip hop is something you live."

♪♪ A Race-Relations-in-America Song: "Fear of a Black Planet"

About the Artists

Public Enemy (PE) is an American hip-hop group that formed in 1982 in Long Island, New York. Much of their early lyrics were heavy with political and socially conscious messages that brought to the fore some of the angst and frustrations of the inner-city black **community**.

Flavor Flav (left) and Chuck D, 2009

In the late eighties, PE introduced a hard, intense sound that changed hip-hop **style**. PE's inventive production team, the Bomb Squad, tailored a unique, noisy, layered avant-garde-inspired sound that incorporated sirens, skittering turntable scratches, and cleverly juxtaposed musical and spoken samples. The group **features** two vocalists with wildly different **styles**: Lead rapper Chuck D, who delivers anti-establishment rhymes in a booming, authoritarian voice, and his sidekick-jester, Flavor Flav, who breaks in with taunts, teases, and questions.

Rolling Stone magazine ranked PE number 44 on its list of the 100 greatest artists of all time—the highest-ranking hip-hop group.

Listen to the song and try to fill in the blanks. You will have two opportunities to hear the song.

Public Enemy—"Fear of a Black Planet"

Man don't you
Worry 'bout a thing
'Bout your daughter
Nope _____ _____ _____ _____
(But supposin' she said she loved me)   5
Are you afraid of the mix of Black and White
We're livin' in a land where
The law say the mixing of race
Makes the blood _____
She's a woman I'm a man   10
Look at your face
I see ya can't stand it

Man you need to _____ _____ don't get mad
I don't need your sistah
(But supposin' she said she loved me)   15
Would you still love her
Or would you dismiss her
What is pure? Who is pure?
Is it European? I ain't sure
If the _____ _____ was to come   20
Thru peace and love
Then what would we be made of?

Excuse us fo'r the news
You might not be amused
But did you know White comes from Black   25
No need to be confused
Excuse us for the news
I question those _____
Why is this fear of Black from White
Influence who you choose?   30

Man, I don't want your wife
Stop screamin' it's not _____ _____ _____ _____ _____
(But supposin' she said she loved me)
What's wrong with some color in your family tree?
I don't know   35

Hey, I'm just a rhyme sayer
Skin protected 'gainst the _____ _____

Breakdown 2001
Might be best to be Black
Or just Brown countdown   40

I've been _____' why
People livin' in fear
Of my shade
(Or my hi-top fade*)
I'm not the one that's runnin'   45
But they got me on the run
Treat me like I have a gun.
All I got is genes and _____
Consider me Black to the bone
All I want is peace and love   50
On this planet
(Ain't that how God planned it?)

Excuse us for the news
You might not be amused
But did you know White comes from Black   55
_____ _____ _____ _____ _____

Excuse us for the news
I question those accused
Why is this fear of Black from White
Influence who you choose?   60

*Song Vocabulary

hi-top fade (noun phrase): a particular type of hairstyle

Listen Again!

Listen to the song again and double-check your answers. When you are finished, check your answers with a partner.

Song Survey

In the last column provide a reason for your choice.

A hi-top fade

1. Were the lyrics easy to understand?	Yes	No	
2. In general, do you like hip-hop music?	Yes	No	
3. Would you listen to more songs by Public Enemy?	Yes	No	
4. Is this the kind of song your parents would listen to?	Yes	No	
5. Do you think songs should address these kinds of serious issues? (Why or why not?)	Yes	No	

Share your answers with a partner.

Song Discussion

 Discuss the following questions in small groups.

1. In Chapter 1, you were introduced to the literary device poetic licence (page 17). Identify some uses of poetic licence in this song, and discuss what effect this has on the listener. Why might Chuck D (the songwriter) have included so many instances of poetic licence?
2. Reread lines 18 and 19. Explain the reference to Europe here. What message is Public Enemy trying to convey with these lines? Do you agree with this message? Why or why not?
3. Reread lines 23 to 28. What is this "news" that is referred to here? Again, what is the message Public Enemy is trying to convey? Do you agree with this message? Why or why not?
4. As you learned in the previous chapter, racism and discrimination is a problem that exists not only in the United States. Nor is it only a problem with respect to the colour of one's skin. What other types of racism exist? Can you think of any examples of racism that are not skin-colour related? Can you think of any examples of racism from your home country? Have you ever experienced racism? Share your thoughts and ideas with your group.

Focus on Listening

Skills Focus: Preparing Questions While Listening

Asking good questions is often just as important as answering them. It demonstrates your ability to synthesize information, shows your interest in a topic, and encourages people to approach a topic from different perspectives or points of view. It also encourages you to be an active listener. Moreover, this skill is multi-functional. You can use it to politely interrupt your instructor, at the end of a presentation, or during a group discussion. You will focus on two key points here:

I. How to think of a question while listening (What should I ask? How should I ask it? When should I ask it?).
II. Some simple phrases or expressions that you can use to introduce your question or request more information.

I. Thinking of a Question While Listening

Read through these listening strategies.
a) Examine the title or topic: What background information will help you understand this topic? Is there any information you might like to know about this topic? Jot this down.
b) Clarity: Are there terms, expressions, or important words that are preventing you from understanding the speaker? Jot down points that will help you remember this section of the talk.
c) Make inferences: Is there an underlying meaning that the speaker is hinting at? Do you want to confirm this? Jot down the inference and ask about it later.
d) Digest and judge: Make a quick evaluation of what was just said, and decide on whether you agree with it or not (make a judgment). If you disagree, jot down why. You can ask about it later.
e) Intonation shift: Listen for major shifts in intonation. This often signals the arrival of important information that might call for clarification. If so, jot it down.
f) Timing: Be aware of the context of the talk. If it's a lecture at a school, don't let too much time pass by before you ask your question. Politely interrupt your professor (see part II) and state your question as clearly as possible. If it's a speech, you should likely wait until the end to ask a question. If it's a discussion, politely interrupt (see part II) and make your enquiry.

Here are some further points to keep in mind:

- You should *always* be listening with a pencil in your hand. Information arrives quickly, and by the time you reach for your pencil the speaker may be on a different point already. It's essential that you be an active and prepared listener.
- Try to make your question as clear and specific as possible (see below).

II. Question Phrases or a Request for More Information

If you're interrupting the speaker, or asking a question after a presentation, try to make eye contact with the speaker and raise your hand. The phrases below will also help you in a discussion:

- "Excuse me / sorry to interrupt / before we move on, can you explain / rephrase / repeat / give another example of…."
- "Can you please explain… in more detail?"
- "How does… work?"
- "Sorry, but what do you mean by…?"
- "Could you tell me more about…?"
- "I don't quite understand what you mean by…. Can you explain that again?"

Skills in Practice

In this chapter's Focus on Speaking exercise below you will be asked to prepare a research presentation on your favourite music genre. When you listen to your classmates' presentations, prepare questions that you can ask them. You should have a pencil in hand while you're listening, and be sure to ask questions at the end. Use the strategies listed to ensure that you are able to both follow their talk *and* prepare questions at the same time.

Focus on Speaking

Skills Focus: Research Presentations, Revisited

In Chapter 3, you studied presentation skills. With a partner discuss any important features of a research presentation that you can recall (How many sections are involved in a presentation? What is the purpose of each section? What are some key phrases involved in giving a presentation?). When you are finished, return to pages 54–57 to review this material.

 Skills in Practice

Prepare a research presentation on your favourite music genre. You may use the presentation you did on a music genre in Chapter 5 as a starting point or guide. Research its history and its influence on society and culture (e.g., electronica's influence on dance music culture, or jazz's influence in shaping the city of New Orleans). While you are preparing this presentation, be sure to follow the advice listed on pages 54–57 of Chapter 3. You should also expect to receive a lot of questions during and / or after your presentation, so be prepared to think on your feet as well (refer back to pages 30–32 of Chapter 2 if you wish to review). Be sure to incorporate as many AWL words in your presentation as possible.

Focus on Reading

Skills Focus: Making Inferences

Making inferences is a skill that you have, no doubt, been doing for almost your entire life. Earlier in this book you were making inferences based on photographs (page 2) and newspaper headlines (pages 59–60), and you have already been asked to make numerous inferences in this chapter. Inferences are not entirely new for you. Let's look at two further examples.

a) You wake up in the morning, gaze at your clock and read that it is 9:30 AM, but you notice that your room is unusually dark. Based on your past experiences, you assume that it's a cloudy day (even though you have yet to look outside). You have just made an inference.

b) You are sitting in your classroom and you hear the sound of a fire truck. Even though you haven't seen the fire (or even the fire truck), you assume that a fire truck is racing toward a fire.

Both of these assumptions, based on previous experiences, are inferences. You reached conclusions without facts being explicitly presented to you (you hadn't seen the clouds yet, nor did you see the fire truck, nor the fire).

With a partner take a minute or two to come up with some more examples of inferences you make in your everyday life. After your discussion, list them below in point form.

1. _____
2. _____
3. _____

When we infer something, we build on a variety of tools. One of the most important of these is context. For example, if in situation (b) above you heard this same sound while sailing alone in the middle of the Pacific Ocean, you probably wouldn't make the same inference. You wouldn't have the context (sitting in a school surrounded by other buildings that could catch on fire, with the potential of fire trucks being around) from which to build an inference. Understanding the context in which a situation exists is essential for making an inference. And the same is true for drawing an inference from written material.

As readers we draw on our own experiences to form inferences. For example:
- i) background knowledge can help us infer ("They couldn't have frozen to death—it was summer");
- ii) knowing about the situation ("Of course everyone was well-dressed—it was a wedding at the palace"); or
- iii) knowing the audience ("He would never say that in front of his mother").

Inferences can also be built around the following:
- iv) common knowledge (rain = umbrellas);
- v) social conventions (say "please" and "thank you");
- vi) shared knowledge (the law of gravity);
- vii) shared experiences (doing chores); and
- viii) shared values (murder is bad).

Consider the following statement:

The senator admitted owning the gun that killed his wife.

This seems like a simple statement about what someone said. Our understanding, however, includes much that is not stated. We can find more meaning inside the words and the phrase. If we look more closely, we can see that the senator was married and his wife is now dead—although this is not actually stated. There are numerous inferences we can draw from this sentence:

- There is a senator.
- He owns a gun.
- He is married.
- His wife is dead.
- A gun caused her death.

Clearly, the original sentence is a clearer and simpler way of conveying all of this information. On a more subtle level, however, we can infer that a public figure (a senator) is involved in a major crime. We can also infer that the gun (or at least a bullet) has probably been recovered and identified as the murder weapon.

We must, however, also recognize the danger of inferences that cannot be made. We do not really know whether the senator is responsible for his wife's death, nor do we know that she died from a gunshot (she could have been hit over the head with the gun). We do not even know if it was murder—it might have been suicide or an accident.

Are we imagining things here? Or are these meanings truly within the sentence? For the most part, we are certainly going beyond what the text *says*, but likely not beyond what it actually *means* to most readers. Inferences such as these are essential for understanding written material. Writers often only hint at what they mean, and mean much more than they actually write. On the other hand, we can see the danger (and temptation) of assuming facts or interpretations for which evidence is not present. We need to recognize that a critical reader reads with an open mind—one that is open to many possible interpretations.

◎ Skills in Practice

Examine this chapter's reading again, and answer the questions below. When you are finished, share your answers with a partner.

1. Paragraph 1: What can you infer about the success of *Fear of a Black Planet*?
2. Paragraph 2: What can you infer about the author's tone* here?
3. Paragraph 4: What can you infer about the irrationality of rap lyrics? How does the word *seem* influence what you might infer from this passage?
4. Paragraph 5: What can you infer about the message of rap music from the perspective of black urban America?
5. Paragraph 6, Line 1: From this sentence, what can you infer about the freedom of rappers to express themselves?
6. Paragraph 7: What can you infer about how white rock music and black rap music is received or accepted by middle-class America?
7. Paragraph 8: What can you infer about the relationship between business and rap music?
8. Paragraph 9: What function does the word *appear* have in sentence 1 with respect to what you might infer from this paragraph?
9. Paragraph 10: What are some inferences you can make regarding the author's position on the successes of black music?
10. Refer back to discussion question 3 on page 96 and answer the question again.

* *Tone* can be described as an author's attitude toward the reader and/or the subject matter. It is often described as "how" something is written (as opposed to "what" is written), or the mood of the piece. For example: *Snakes are nasty creatures!* The choice of the word *nasty* suggests a negative tone. The use of the exclamation mark (!) suggests an even stronger, negative attitude toward snakes. You could argue here that the tone is both negative and aggressive. (Accordingly, you can also infer that the writer is not fond of snakes.)

Focus on Writing

Skills Focus: Editing and Proofreading

The skills presented in this section may be the most important ones that you will learn in this book. Editing and proofreading your writing is essential in order to produce the best possible work you can for your instructor. Even if your research is fantastic, a poorly written paper will likely produce a very poor grade. These skills provide an important step in learning to write well. These suggestions for improving your writing are not unique—both English language learners and native English speakers around the world practise these skills. The tips below, some of which come from The Writing Center at the University of North Carolina at Chapel Hill, can be applied in three ways: to both editing and proofreading, to the editing process, and to the proofreading process. With each of the following headings are a list of suggestions and tips. Pay close attention to these and apply them to your own writing.

I.   Editing and Proofreading
      Before examining each skill separately, read these tips that apply to both editing and proofreading:

- *"Get some distance from the text!* It's hard to edit or proofread a paper that you've just finished writing—it's still too familiar, and you will tend to skip over a lot of errors. Put the paper aside for a few hours, days, or weeks….
- *Decide what medium lets you proofread most carefully*. Some people like to work right at the computer, while others like to sit back with a printed copy that they can mark up as they read.
- *Try changing the look of your document*. Altering the size, spacing, colour, or style of the text may trick your brain into thinking it's seeing an unfamiliar document, and that can help you get a different perspective on what you've written.
- *Find a quiet place to work*. Don't try to do your proofreading in front of the TV…. Find a place where you can concentrate and avoid distractions.
- *If possible, do your editing and proofreading in several short blocks of time*, rather than all at once—otherwise, your concentration is likely to wane."

II.   The Editing Process
      After you finish your first essay draft, you should begin the editing process. You should be editing for a variety of things:

- "Content—Have you done everything the assignment requires? Are the claims you make accurate? If it is required to do so, does your paper make an argument? Is the argument complete? Are all of your claims consistent? Have you supported each point with adequate evidence? ….
- Overall structure—Does your paper have an appropriate introduction and conclusion? Is your thesis clearly stated in your introduction? Is it clear how each paragraph in the body of your paper is related to your thesis? Are the paragraphs arranged in a logical sequence? Have you made clear transitions between paragraphs? ….
- Clarity—Have you defined any important terms that might be unclear to your reader? Is the meaning of each sentence clear? … Is it clear what each pronoun (he, she, it, they, which, who, this, etc.) refers to? ….
- Style—Have you used an appropriate tone (formal, informal, persuasive, etc.)? … Have you varied the length and structure of your sentences?"
- Citations—Are ideas, quotations, and paraphrases that you found from outside material cited? Did you cite correctly, according to the style guide appropriate for your class?

In general, pay attention to your own patterns of error; understanding the mistakes that you make frequently will be helpful for editing future papers that you write.

III. The Proofreading Process

Proofreading is the last stage of your essay writing before you hand your work in to your instructor for grading. Here, you should focus on mechanical errors such as grammatical, spelling, and punctuation problems. Each of you will develop a preference for how you go about proofreading. Experiment with the suggestions below until you find a proofreading style that works for you. Once you have found a system you like, stick with it. The more familiar you become with one particular proofreading style, the easier it will be to identify errors in the future.

- *Take your time when you proofread.* Proofreading will likely take hours. A fast read will allow you to see only the most obvious problems. Create a writing plan that will give you ample time to proofread your work.
- *A computer's grammar- and spell-checker is NOT reliable.* It often misses errors, or suggests corrections that are incorrect.
- *Choose ONLY one item to proofread for at a time.* For example, proofread for punctuation only. Then go back and proofread for subject-verb agreement, and then articles, and then something else, until you are satisfied with your work. You will have a much easier time identifying errors when you are search for them one at a time. (See the Appendix, page 185 for an example.)
- *Read your essay out loud.* This will help you hear how the words you have written sound together, and will help you hear awkward phrases, grammatical structures, or punctuation, for example.
- *Pay attention to every punctuation mark, one at a time.* This will force you to look at each one, and to question its accuracy.
- *If something looks or sounds odd to you, there is probably a problem.* Do not ignore this—research the potential error.

Proofreading and editing are skills that require practice. In time, you will become more efficient at identifying your errors, and in turn, producing better writing. Focus on developing a proofreading and editing strategy that works best for you. Once this is in place, you can focus more of your attention on improving the quality of the content of your writing.

Skills in Practice

In Chapter 5, you wrote a paper about education and apartheid. Using the skills you have just read about, return to that essay and both edit and proofread it. By now you will have had some time away from this essay. As such, the first suggestion listed on page 107 (get some distance from the text) has already been accomplished. Consult the first five points again, and then begin the editing process. Once that is complete, make the necessary corrections and print your paper again. Finally, refer to the proofreading section above and proofread your paper.

Additional Vocabulary

Word	Part of Speech	Definition	Sample Sentence

The Stolen Generation

Introduction

Track 7: Aboriginal History

This chapter deals with the indigenous people of Australia—the Aborigines.

Listen to a very brief overview of Aboriginal history. Take notes and summarize the contents of this overview with your partner. Use some of the skills you already studied thus far to help you with your summary.

When you are finished sharing your summary, study the diagram below.

In the talk the narrator talked about the "dreamtime." What kind of things can you infer about dreamtime and its relation to Aboriginal culture from this diagram?

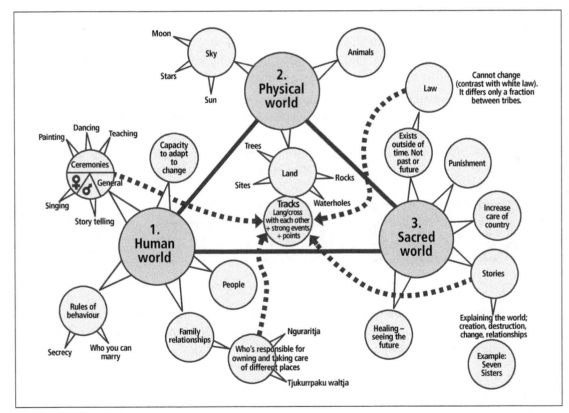

The Dreamtime Chart

Previewing the Reading

Preview the reading by examining the timeline on the next page. With a partner or in a small group, go through each date and discuss what significance it might have for Aboriginal people and their history in Australia.

55,000 BCE	— Conclusive data indicating arrival of Aboriginal people in Australia.
1451–1900 CE	— Trade with Asia (Dutch documents record trade between Indonesian sailors and Aborigines).
1788	— Britain established its penal colony in Port Jackson (Sydney).
1790	— Protectionist policies implemented, restricting Aborigines' right to free movement to specific areas such as reserves or missions.
1820s	— The Black Wars: a struggle for land between indigenous groups and Europeans along settlement frontiers.
1830s	— Colonies are established based on British law.
1850s–1970s	— The policy of removing Aboriginal children from their families begins.
1880	— About 200 Aboriginal children enrolled in public schools. (In the 1900s, Aboriginal schools are established following requests by the white community to exclude Aboriginal children from public schools.)
1901	— Australia becomes a nation. Indigenous people are not considered citizens.
1911	— The Aborigines Protection Act passed (confines indigenous people to reserves).
1936	— The beginning of assimilation policies (meaning that all persons of Aboriginal birth or mixed blood in Australia are required to live in the same manner as white Australians).
1960s	— The start of the modern land-rights movement and the widespread awakening by non-Aboriginal Australians to indigenous claims for justice.
1962	— Voting is extended to all indigenous people.
1972	— The policy of self-determination is adopted by the government, replacing earlier policies of protectionism and assimilation.
1995–97	— The National Inquiry into the Separation of Aboriginal and Torres Strait Islander Children from their Families was held, culminating in the 1997 report *Bringing Them Home*.
2008	— Then-Australian prime minister Kevin Rudd issues an official apology to families torn apart because of the policy of assimilation.

ⓐ The Stolen Generation

Academic Word List (AWL) Vocabulary

The following AWL words will appear in this chapter's reading. Before completing the following exercise, skim the reading with a focus on the words in bold print. This will help you complete the table, and will prepare you for the reading.

compensate	behalf	contract	assume
notion	immigration	reliance	consume
abnormal	generation	restrict	removal
ultimately	eliminate	adult	abandon
welfare	so-called	design	affect
adequately	federal	chapter	successive
implementation	source	final	decline
expose	psychology	initiate	channel
conform	adapt		

Place each of the AWL words under the appropriate heading in the chart below. Use a dictionary if you need help.

Noun	Verb	Noun & Verb	Adjective	Adverb	Noun & Adjective

The Stolen Generation at a Glance...

1   Inhabitants of Australia, prior to the arrival of European settlers, lived without what colonizers would describe as a recognizable system of government, land ownership, **contracts**, trade, or religion, for tens of thousands of years. Despite their lengthy presence on the island, in 1788 the British declared Australia "terra nullius"—a land without people.

2   This preposterous **assumption** continues to scar the Aboriginal people today. As a result of this British declaration, the land that the indigenous people find sacred has been developed for its natural resources and raped of its spiritual significance. Although the Aboriginal people failed to share with Europeans in the notion of private property, they were in fact very territorial and depended upon the land for their physical, **psychological**, and spiritual well-being.

Causalities of Colonialism

3   Alienated from their ancestral land, **exposed** to foreign diseases such as smallpox, tuberculosis, and influenza brought by **immigration**, and their **sources** of food eliminated by European farming methods and animals imported by Europeans into Australia (such as the fox, rabbit, and feral cat), Aborigines eventually became **reliant** on European colonizers for their day-to-day survival. Forced to **consume** nontraditional foods **abnormally** high in sugar and starches, obesity and malnutrition were coupled with the negative effects of alcohol.

The Stolen **Generations**

4   Based on **notions** of Darwinism and a **declining** Aboriginal population, in the early 1900s many in the Australian government **assumed** that the Aboriginal people were dying out. As such, "protection" policies were created. In essence, however, these were policies of segregation and **restrictions**. Due to the belief that the full-blooded Aboriginal race would soon disappear anyway, the Australian government created the policy of "assimilation," wherein an attempt was made to breed out Aboriginal blood. This policy allowed for the forced **removal** of Aboriginal children from their families, where they were then enrolled in government institutions and expected to **conform** to European values and embrace a "white" ideology. It was hoped that they would, in turn, breed with whites; this was **designed** to **ultimately eliminate** the Aboriginal bloodline. **Adult** Aborigines were, instead, sent to work camps and religious missions, where it was hoped they too would **abandon** their distinct culture and **adapt** a white ideology.

5   It is unclear how many children were **channelled** into assimilation, as most records have been lost or destroyed. Many parents whose children were taken never saw them again, and siblings who were taken were deliberately separated from each other. Today, many Aboriginal people still do not know who their relatives are or have been unable to track them down. The **generations** of children who were taken from their families became known as the Stolen **Generations**. The practice of **removing** children continued up until the late 1960s.

6   As the 1960s arrived, Aborigines began to fight for more land rights and improved living conditions. Following these public protests, the notion of "assimilation" became increasingly ridiculed, until it was abandoned. In 1967, a referendum granted Aborigines citizenship to Australia, a land they had already occupied thousands of years previous.

Bringing Them Home

7   In the 1990s, the Human Rights and Equal Opportunity Commission **initiated** a national inquiry into the practice of **removing** children. The National Inquiry into the Separation of Aboriginal and Torres Strait Islander Children produced the report *Bringing Them Home*, which was presented to the Australian parliament on 26 May 1997. The report outlined the devastating impact the child-**removal** policies had on children and their families. It found that many of the institutions and homes in which the children were placed were very cruel, and sexual and physical abuse of the children was common. The report told a story of **welfare** boards, of segregation, and of **so-called** assimilation policies that did not work. The report also told stories of mothers fleeing into the bush with their babies, of the virtual slavery of the young girls who were sent out to rural properties to work as maids, and of nannies of the children being treated like cattle. One woman reported: "We was bought like a market. We was all lined up in white dresses and they would come round and pick you out like you was for sale [sic]."

8   The report found that the practice of forced **removal** was highly traumatic not only for the children, but also for their families. The policy broke important cultural, spiritual, and family ties that crippled individuals, whole families, and even entire communities. The report found that members of the Stolen **Generations** suffered higher rates of sexual abuse, maltreatment, dislocation of family life, poverty, and hardship than other Aboriginal people.

9   The report also found that the policy of forced **removal** was based on racist **assumptions** about the benefits that would flow from such **policies**. The aim of the policy was to "breed out" the Aboriginal race. In international law, practices **designed** to destroy an entire race of people are known as "genocide," and are forbidden under the 1948 Convention on Prevention and Punishment of the Crime of Genocide. While many records have been lost, it is estimated that 100,000 indigenous people have been **affected** by the policy of **removal**.

National Apology

10   While many Aboriginal groups feel they can never be **adequately compensated** for the loss of their families, since the *Bringing Them Home* report was released, there has been a strong campaign for an official apology from the Australian government. This was one of the report's key recommendations, along with financial **compensation** for the suffering inflicted by the government.

11   In 1997, Prime Minister John Howard refused to make an official apology. He argued that the current **generation** should not be responsible for the mistakes of the past. Aboriginal rights activists argued that it was important to recognize the truth of Australia's history if indigenous people are to deal with it and move forward in reconciliation. In 2007, a new government was elected, and promised to **finally** make an official apology to the Stolen **Generations**. At the first

session of the new **federal** parliament, on 13 February 2008, Prime Minister Kevin Rudd **issued** an official apology to the Stolen **Generations** on **behalf** of the government. The following remarks formed a part of his speech:

> Today we honour the Indigenous peoples of this land, the oldest continuing cultures in human history.
>
> We reflect on their past mistreatment.
>
> We reflect in particular on the mistreatment of those who were Stolen **Generations**—this blemished **chapter** in our nation's history.
>
> The time has now come for the nation to turn a new page in Australia's history by righting the wrongs of the past and so moving forward with confidence to the future.
>
> We apologise for the laws and policies of **successive** Parliaments and governments that have inflicted profound grief, suffering and loss on these our fellow Australians.
>
> We apologise especially for the **removal** of Aboriginal and Torres Strait Islander children from their families, their communities and their country.
>
> For the pain, suffering and hurt of these Stolen **Generations**, their descendants and for their families left behind, we say sorry.
>
> To the mothers and the fathers, the brothers and the sisters, for the breaking up of families and communities, we say sorry.
>
> And for the indignity and degradation thus inflicted on a proud people and a proud culture, we say sorry.

12 Members of the Stolen **Generations** were invited onto the floor of parliament and to watch the apology from the gallery. The majority of Australians welcomed the apology and celebrations were held across the country. Some **sections** of the community and the media still strongly opposed the apology, arguing that the people who took the children thought they were doing the "right thing," that children were taken for their own good, that the government should not be responsible for the past, and that the apology would lead to a flood of **compensation** claims. During the apology, the prime minister ruled out financial **compensation** for the Stolen **Generations**, but reconfirmed the government's commitment to focus on "closing the gap"—to raise the health of indigenous people so it matches those of other Australians. The campaign continues for **compensation** for members of the Stolen **Generations**, and for the full **implementation** of the recommendations of the *Bringing Them Home* report.

Fill in the table below with three words from this article that are *not* from the AWL, but that are new for you.

Word	Part of Speech	Definition	Sample Sentence

Share your table with a partner.

Reading for Details

The following statements are incorrect. Correct them on the lines below.

1. Even though Britain noted systems of a "civilized" society, they still declared Australia "terra nullius."

_____

2. The policy of assimilation was against the forced removal of Aboriginal children from their families.

_____

3. The policy of forced removal was based on the fact that more good than bad would result from such actions.

_____

4. During the 13 February 2008 apology, the prime minister of Australia encouraged families affected by this tragedy to seek financial compensation.

_____

Share your answers with a partner. Try to use this chapter's AWL vocabulary as often as you can.

Discussion Questions

◉ Discuss the following questions with a partner.

1. As in Chapter 5, here is another example of British colonialism. Why might the British have been interested in Australia? What benefits could be derived from colonizing here?
2. Note the word *assimilation* in paragraph 4. Why is it in quotation marks (" ") and what significance does this have?
3. Note the second sentence of paragraph 11. Why might Howard have made this statement? Do you agree with him? Why, or why not?
4. Reread the portion of the speech Rudd made. Is this a thorough enough apology? Or should he have said more? What else could he have added?

Vocabulary Practice

Definitions

Match the words below with their appropriate definitions.

Words	Definitions
1. behalf 2. affect 3. notion 4. reliant 5. expose 6. conform 7. so-called 8. federal	_____ to show something that is usually hidden
	_____ an idea, a belief, or an understanding of something
	_____ to behave and think in the same way as most other people in a group or society; to agree with or match something
	_____ used to show that you do not think that the word or phrase that is being used to describe somebody / something is appropriate
	_____ as the representative of somebody or instead of them; in order to help somebody; because of somebody; for somebody
	_____ connected with national government rather than the local government of an individual state
	_____ to produce a change in somebody / something
	_____ needing somebody / something in order to survive, be successful, etc.

Definitions taken or adapted from *Oxford Advanced Learner's Dictionary 8th Edition* by A. S. Hornby © Oxford University Press 2010. Reproduced by permission.

Check a learner's dictionary for the difference between *affect* and *effect*. Native English speakers often confuse the two, especially in their writing. On the lines below provide a clear definition of each, as well as a sample sentence that will help you remember the difference.

1. affect

   _____

   _____

2. effect

   _____

   _____

⊚ Expanding Lexical Concepts

Collocations

Use the AWL vocabulary in the text box to form high-frequency collocations with the words below.

adapt	restriction	immigration
chapter	psychology	eliminate
adult	removal	
contract	welfare	

1. long-term, permanent, short-term, written, verbal, lucrative, employment, service, marriage, bid for / negotiate / draw up / write / conclude / enter into / break a _____

2. illegal, large-scale, mass, pass through _____; _____ control, law, policy, rules, officer, official, service

3. severe, tight, proposed, contractual, government, legal, age, parking, travel, visa, impose / introduce / place a _____

4. young, single, consenting, responsible _____; _____ life, education, literacy, population

5. animal, child, community, personal _____; _____ state, department, services, system, officer, clinic, facilities, payments

6. introductory, opening, difficult, sad, unhappy _____

7. clinical, professional, experimental, developmental, educational, child, group, human

   _____

8. altogether, completely, entirely, totally, virtually, effectively, seek / take steps / try / be designed to _____

9. quickly, easily, readily, be able / unable to, need / find it difficult / hard to _____; _____ successfully, well, accordingly

10. complete, total, temporary, successful, immediate, arrange for, demand, seek, facilitate

    _____

Using Collocations

Fill in the blanks using the AWL word in parentheses with the correct collocation from the list on page 117. More than one answer may be suitable at times.

1. Herd psychology, or _____, refers to a large mass of people who usually behave in the same manner. (psychology)

2. When entering a new country you are often required to _____ first. (immigration)

3. _____ agencies are designed to protect the well-being of young children. (welfare)

4. The increase in the _____ of countries like Japan is causing serious economic strain. (adult)

5. Some computer programs are designed to _____ software viruses. (eliminate)

6. Before _____, both parties should be aware of any compensation provided for early dismissals. (contract)

7. Many countries impose an _____ on the consumption of alcohol. (restriction)

8. The death of her father concluded a _____ in her life. (chapter)

9. Many people _____ to new cultures in a short period of time, adding to an already stressful period in their lives. (adapt)

10. The newly formed government called for an _____ of the military chief. (removal)

Word Forms

Fill in the blanks with the appropriate form of the AWL vocabulary.

1. Based on the following _____, the adult population of shark species in the wild is expected to decline in the next decade.
   a) assume   b) assumption   c) assuming   d) assumed

2. The amount of abnormal test results based on previous studies is in _____.
   a) declining   b) declined   c) declines   d) decline

3. As the ship began to sail beyond the horizon, the full weight of _____ fell upon the shoulders of the stranded islanders.
   a) abandonment   b) abandoning   c) abandoned   d) abandons

4. Fashion _____ the world over are meeting in New York this week.
   a) designer   b) designing   c) designers   d) designed

5. When blood pressure is _____ high, it is best to contact a physician.
   a) normal   b) normalized   c) normally   d) abnormally

6. _____ levels in the United States are presently at an unsustainable level.
   a) Consuming   b) Consumed   c) Consumer   d) Consumption

7. Victims of last winter's hurricane were not adequately _____ for the damage sustained to their homes.
   a) compensate   b) compensation   c) compensated   d) compensation

8. The line of _____ to any royal throne usually follows a family bloodline.
   a) succession   b) successor   c) successions   d) successive

9. In order to _____ any new law, it must first pass through a series of rigorous debates.
   a) implementation   b) implemented   c) implement   d) implements

10. If the government wants to channel further funds into existing programs, it must first ensure that an _____ infrastructure is in place to support them.
    a) adequately   b) adequate   c) inadequate   d) inadequately

Before Moving On...
About Folk-Rock

In Chapter 3, you reviewed folk music (page 48). Use the information there to help you write a brief summary of this music genre. (Try to do this without referring back to Chapter 1, where folk music was first introduced; if this is too difficult and you need to return to Chapter 1, ensure that you write your summary in *your own* words).

_____

_____

_____

_____

_____

_____

_____

A Stolen-Generation Song: "Took the Children Away"

About the Artist

Archie Roach, a member of the Stolen Generations, was born in Australia, in 1956. As a child he was forcibly removed from his family and frequently changed foster homes*. In his teens he received a letter from a sister he didn't know he had. This sparked an angry search for his identity and his place in the world.

In 1990 Roach recorded his first record, *Charcoal Lane*. The message therein, reaching out to Australians and the world, was that despite the neglect and misery he was put through, his connection to the land and culture of his ancestors remains strong. The album contained "Took the Children Away," a song that deals with Roach's experience as one of the Stolen Generations. Roach, a storyteller in the tradition of his ancestors, continues to sing of intimate real-life stories that have touched the heart and soul of audiences around the world.

Listen to the song and try to fill in the blanks. You will have two opportunities to hear the song.

Archie Roach—"Took the Children Away"

This story's right, this story's true
I would not tell _____ to you
Like the promises they did not keep
And how they fenced us in like _____.
Said to us come take our hand   5
Set us up on _____ _____.
Taught us to read, to write and pray
Then they took the children away,
Took the children away,
The children away.   10
_____ from their mother's breast
Said this is for the best
Took them away.

The welfare and the policeman
Said _____ _____ _____ _____   15
We'll give to them what you can't give
Teach them how to really live.
Teach them how to live they said
Humiliated* them instead
Taught them that and taught them this   20
And others taught them _____.
You took the children away
The children away
Breaking their mother's heart
Tearing us all apart   25
Took them away

One dark day on Framlingham*
Came and _____ _____ _____ _____
My mother cried go get their dad
He came running, fightin' mad   30
Mother's tears were falling down
Dad shaped up and _____ _____ _____.
He said "You touch my kids and you fight me"
And they took us from our family.
Took us away   35
They took us away
_____ from our mother's breast
Said this is for the best
Took us away.

Told us what to do and say   40
Told us all the _____ _____ _____
Then they split us up again
And gave us gifts to ease the pain
Sent us off to foster homes*
As we grew up _____ _____ _____   45
'Cause we were acting white
Yet feeling black

One sweet day all the children came back
The children come back

The children come back   50
Back where their hearts _____ _____
Back where they all belong
The children came back
Said the children came back
The children came back   55
Back where they understand
Back to their _____ _____
The children came back

Back to their mother
Back to their father   60
Back to their sister
Back to their brother
Back to their _____
Back to their _____
All the children come back   65
The children came back
The children came back
Yes, I came back.

*Song Vocabulary

humiliate (verb): to make somebody feel ashamed or stupid and lose the respect of other people
Framlingham (noun): an Aboriginal reserve in Victoria, Australia that closed in 1916
foster home (noun): a household in which an orphaned or delinquent child is placed (usually by a social-service agency)

The definition of *humiliate* taken from *Oxford Advanced Learner's Dictionary 8th Edition* by A. S. Hornby. © Oxford University Press 2010. Reproduced by permission.

Listen Again!

Listen to the song again and double-check your answers. When you are finished, check your answers with a partner.

Song Survey

In the last column provide a reason for your choice.

1. Were the lyrics easy to understand?	Yes	No	
2. Would you listen to more songs by Archie Roach?	Yes	No	
3. Is this the kind of song your parents would listen to?	Yes	No	
4. Now that you know the background story to this song, would you recommend it to your friends?	Yes	No	
5. Do you think music is a good way to inform people about serious problems and situations in the world?	Yes	No	

Share your answers with a partner.

Song Discussion

Discuss the following questions in small groups.

1. What was the strongest emotion you felt while listening to this song? Why? What qualities of the song (the lyrics, the musician's voice, the story behind the song, etc.) may have made you feel like this?

2. Discuss the significance of the pronoun *I* in relation to the song. Why do you think it is used only at the beginning and end of the song? Why might this pronoun be positioned in this manner?

3. a) Reread lines 7, 17, 18, 41, and 42. What can you infer about the British attitude toward Aboriginal people at that time?

   b) If the British considered themselves culturally and morally superior, why might they have treated people like this? Is there a sense of hypocrisy here? Why or why not?

4. Reread line 19. Think of a time in your life where you were humiliated. Describe the situation and your emotions in as much detail as you can.

Focus on Listening

Skills Review: Note-taking Skills and Listening for Gist and Details

The listening skills you have learned thus far should help you comfortably sit through longer lectures. Adjusting yourself to longer periods of active listening is essential for your continued academic success. Lectures often range from 30 minutes to three hours. Training yourself to sit through such long periods of intense concentration is not easy, but it is necessary. Read the following advice from a one-time college student:

> You can't escape the lecture. You can't get around it; the lecture is still the most common form of instruction in college. It's a fact of your life right now. The typical college student will sit through literally hundreds of hours of lectures during an undergraduate career. Most students actually stay awake throughout these lectures; many even listen hard and try to learn. And yet, only a relative few ever develop an adequate system for taking good lecture notes. Meanwhile, the many students who take terrible notes wonder why they don't do better on exams.
>
> Fact: Good note-taking skills are essential for good academic progress!
>
> Of course, there's no one perfect system for taking good lecture notes, and nearly everybody develops some personal code of abbreviations, patterns, and outline forms.

Take a few minutes to review all of the listening skills you have studied thus far (pages 12–14, 53–54, 68–69, 88–89, and 103–4). Each chapter presents you with a skill that can be adapted to a classroom-lecture environment. When you have finished reviewing them, discuss each item with a partner. How are they similar or different? How can each be beneficial in a lecture setting? What do you do differently that helps form your own system of note-taking? Share your ideas.

In the following exercise, combine all of the listening skills and strategies you have learned and use them to develop your own pattern or system of note-taking. Once you become comfortable with a pattern maintain it, regardless of what kind of class you are taking—the system you develop should work well in any lecture environment (review page 183 in the Appendix again for an example).

Skills in Practice
Track 8: Australian Aborigines—First People in the Americas?

You are about to listen to a lecture about the first humans to arrive in the Americas (North and South America). The lecture itself is introduced in the form of a radio program, or interview, but then continues on in lecture format.

Before the lecture begins, study the map and the photos below to build context for the lecture. Based on the data below, what do you expect to hear in this lecture? Discuss this with a partner.

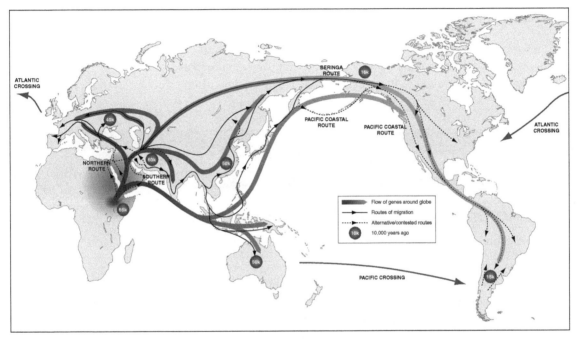

Migration map of modern humans

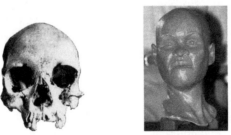

Luzia's skull, unearthed in Brazil, and a constructed model of what she may have looked like

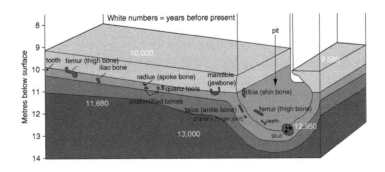

The location where Luzia's remains were found in Lapa Vermelha, Brazil

Pre-Listening Vocabulary

red tape (noun): official rules that seem more complicated than necessary and prevent things from being done quickly

DNA (noun): deoxyribonucleic acid (the chemical in the cells of animals and plants that carries genetic information)

genome (noun): the complete set of genes in a cell or living thing

Definitions taken or adapted from Oxford Advanced Learner's Dictionary 8th Edition by A. S. Hornby © Oxford University Press 2010. Reproduced by permission.

Listen to the lecture and take notes. (Remember that you should be beginning to develop your own note-taking style now.) When the lecture is over you will be given a short quiz based on the lecture.

I. When you are finished, review your notes and ensure that you can understand them. Take a few minutes to rewrite anything and make sure that they are organized.

II. Compare your notes with those of a partner. Fill in any important information that you are missing.

Focus on Writing and Reading

Writing Skills Focus: Unity and Coherence

Unity and coherence can be discussed at two levels: the paragraph and the essay.

Unity

Having unity is important at both the paragraph and essay levels. A paragraph is unified when all of its sentences work toward the same end. Each phrase and sentence should illustrate, clarify, explain, support, and / or address the idea that the topic sentence puts forward. (For a review of Topic Sentences, see page 18 of Chapter 1.) An essay is unified when all of the paragraphs illustrate, clarify, explain, support, and / or address the idea expressed in the essay's thesis statement. (For a review of Thesis Statements, see pages 36–37 of Chapter 2). There may, of course, be more than one idea in a paragraph or an essay, but all of them should be focused on one overall theme.

Coherence

Paragraph or essay coherence is strongest when your writing (both within paragraphs and in your essay as a whole) is organized in a logical manner (idea / point / example A / example B / example C / example D / conclusion), and the writing itself moves along this clear path.

There are several ways a paragraph or essay may lose coherence. Be careful to avoid the following:

1. an excessive use of short, choppy sentences.
2. an illogical arrangement of ideas or sentences.
3. lack of transitions or use of the wrong transitions. (Transitions, when used properly, help contribute to the flow of your writing.)

Transitions

Below are two lists. On the right is a list of transition words and phrases. On the left is a list of when best to use these transitions. Study these lists, and then match the transitions on the right with how best to use them on the left.

1. _____ to give examples

2. _____ to give additional information

3. _____ to show how things are related in space

4. _____ to show how things are related in time

5. _____ to show contrast

6. _____ to show comparison

7. _____ to show results

8. _____ to show summary

a) above, below, here, there, opposite

b) similarly, also, in the same way, likewise, in the same manner

c) in summary, hence, in conclusion, finally, all in all

d) for example, specifically, for instance, thus, to illustrate, namely

e) also, further, in addition, moreover, and

f) thus, therefore, as a result, consequently, to this end

g) but, however, in contrast, on the other hand, even so

h) after, before, meanwhile, in the past, later

Study the following poorly written paragraph.

> Canadian software companies face several tough challenges in the new millennium because of "brain drain," the weak Canadian dollar, and the monopoly held by their American counterparts. In contrast, the Canadian dollar continues its downward spiral even today. Brain drain is a bad thing. Our greatest resources are leaving. In the same way, Microsoft is squeezing out its competitors. In comparison, if the brain drain continues, Canadian companies will find it difficult to produce innovative software. The weak dollar will hurt us. It will help Americans.

Identify two or three serious problems with this paragraph. When you are finished, discuss these problems (and their solutions) with a partner. Afterwards, rewrite this paragraph in a much more coherent and unified fashion. Don't forget to include the appropriate transitions.

_____
_____
_____
_____
_____
_____
_____

Early in this chapter (page 119) you wrote a paragraph about folk music. Using the skills noted on the previous pages, rewrite that paragraph. Be sure to include a topic sentence and the necessary transitions. Write a clear, well-organized paragraph that is both unified and coherent.

_____
_____
_____
_____
_____
_____

Reading Skills Focus: Synthesizing Material into a Coherent Unit

There are times when you will need to synthesize material from multiple sources in order to effectively answer an exam question or to write a paper. For example, you may be asked to examine a graph and an article on a related topic and to combine the information each provides into a quality answer. You will have to draw on the important points of each text and produce a single, coherent paragraph or essay. Synthesizing material requires that you ask a few questions about the material you are examining.

1. What does the question ask of me? What does my instructor want me to do or to synthesize? (See Chapter 4, pages 69–70 for a review of how to read an exam question.)
2. What do the materials have in common? Do they express the same facts? Do they provide different support for the same idea? Do they express things differently (graphs, charts, lists, examples, pictures, etc.)?
3. After I've sorted through the material, what points can I synthesize or bring together to answer the question?

Once this is completed you need to think about actually writing your answer. You will need to develop a thesis statement for an essay-style response (see Chapter 2, pages 36–37), or a topic sentence for an expository paragraph–style response (see Chapter 1, pages 17–19). When this is finished you should begin writing a rough draft, following the writing skills noted regarding unity and coherence. Next, you should review your answer when it is completed keeping in mind the proofreading and editing skills you learned in Chapter 6 (pages 107–8).

You are likely becoming aware of the growing tendency in this book to constantly force you back to previous chapters in order to refresh your memory regarding different skills. This is called "recycling." All of the skills in this book need to be practised many times—practising them only once will not allow you to master them. Like any skill, you need to be constantly reviewing them and practising them over and over again.

Skills in Practice

Study the map and diagram from the Focus on Listening section. Along with your notes from the earlier lecture synthesize the material to answer the questions below. Use the points discussed above to help you out. You should answer each question with a high-quality, expository paragraph that clearly and coherently answers the question.

1. Three theories are posited for how the Aborigines may have arrived in South America. Summarize these theories in a clear and concise paragraph.
2. Of the three theories discussed in question 1, which do you think is the most plausible? Choose one and demonstrate why this is the most likely theory. In doing so, be sure to trace the path of migration.
3. Outline how Luzia was discovered, and when she was alive. Explain how scientists know this.

Focus on Speaking

Skills Focus: Informal Debates

Formal debates often follow strict rules of time and format. In a common, everyday academic setting, however, debating formats are rarely used. Having said that, the skills that are required of a successful debater *are the same* skills that are necessary on a daily basis in an academic setting. You have already studied some of these skills: summarizing key points (Chapter 1, pages 14–15), thinking on your feet (Chapter 2, pages 30–32), summarizing events while demonstrating critical thinking (Chapter 4, page 67), and defending a point of view (Chapter 5, pages 90–91). Often, all of these skills need to be processed together at the same time. Here are some instances where this might be required:

1. a tutorial (a formal study group that reviews the contents of the class lecture)

2. a study group (you may be asked for your opinion—and to explain it)

3. another student questions a comment you make in class

4. an instructor asks you for more information, or for an example to explain your point

5. arguing in the cafeteria with your friends about good music

6. being asked for clarification about a point you make during a job interview

7. defending a decision to your parents / teachers / friends / peers

As you can see, these skills move well beyond the academic environment. In general, they will help you express your ideas more clearly on an everyday basis.

One of the best ways to practise putting all of the skills listed above to use is by actually having informal debates. The goal of this is threefold:

1. to improve your language skills
2. to improve your critical thinking skills
3. to increase the speed of goals 1 and 2 (Classmates and instructors, as well as your friends, will not patiently wait all day for your reply—you need to get used to processing information in English at a much faster rate.)

Spend a few minutes reviewing the skills listed above. Turn back to where they were studied and go over them carefully. When you are finished, discuss the most important features of each skill with a partner or small group.

Although most of the debates you will practise are informal, they will need a basic structure. Follow these easy steps to ensure the maximum benefit from your time studying this:

1. divide yourselves into groups of four (two people arguing against two people)
2. ensure that one pair supports one idea, while the other is in opposition
3. follow the diagram on the next page, beginning at the top of the circle

You may notice that in this design, there is really no clear way of determining the winner of the discussion. That is not, however, the point. Remember to stay focused on your goals: improving your language skills, improving your critical thinking skills, and improving the speed at which you process both of these.

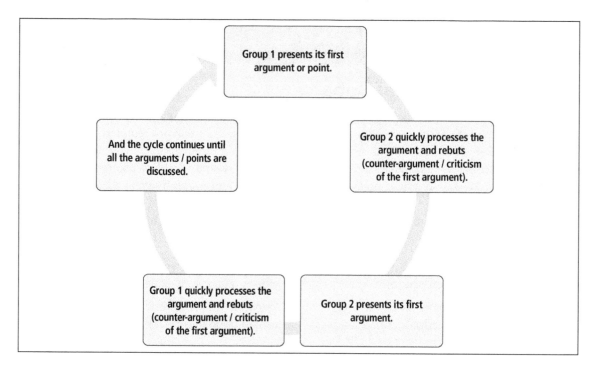

Skills in Practice

◎ Exercise A

Using the format outlined above, debate the following statements:

Statement	Group 1	Group 2
Classical music is better than rock.	Support classical music and criticize rock.	Criticize classical music and support rock.
Winter holidays are better than summer holidays.	Support winter holidays and criticize summer holidays.	Criticize winter holidays and support summer holidays.
Studying a musical instrument is better than playing a sport.	Support studying a musical instrument and criticize playing a sport.	Criticize studying a musical instrument and support playing a sport.
Choose a topic of your group's choice.		

◎ Exercise B

The following debate topic will require intensive research. In the Focus on Listening and Focus on Writing sections in this chapter, you were introduced to the idea that Aboriginals were the first to possibly settle in the Americas. This is not the only new theory that is changing the way people think about the more recent history of the Americas. Some writers and scholars are also challenging the traditional theory that Christopher Columbus was the first to discover the modern Americas. Some scholars are putting forward the idea that the Chinese first discovered America about 70 years before Columbus did. Which group of scholars is correct: the traditionalists, who believe Columbus discovered the Americas in 1492, or the new group of scholars that suggest the Chinese discovered the Americas in 1421? In your groups, decide which theory you will argue in favour of and prepare accordingly.

Note: With debates such as this, where you have ample time to prepare, it is imperative that you think about what the other group might say. This should be done in advance, as part of your preparation. In this manner you will be well prepared to criticize their position and to defend your own.

Additional Vocabulary

Word	Part of Speech	Definition	Sample Sentence

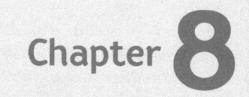

Chapter 8

Science and Crime

CRIME SCEN

Introduction

In the previous chapter, you were introduced to DNA (page 124). Read what one newscaster noted regarding its discovery:

The discovery of DNA is considered one of the most important events of the twentieth century and the study of DNA continues to provide assistance in a number of ways including medicine, forensics, and genealogy.

◉ Study the information below regarding DNA. When you are finished create a list with a partner outlining possible uses of DNA. How might understanding human DNA be beneficial for society? How might it be harmful?

A DNA molecule consists of two long strands that twist around each other like a spiral staircase. Each strand consists of a backbone of ribose (a sugar) together with phosphate groups and nitrogen bases.

There are four different nitrogen bases: adenine (A), thymine (T), cytosine (C) and guanine (G). These bases are often called after their first letter. The A in a strand can form bonds with the T in the opposite strand and the G can form bonds with the C. These form base pairs:

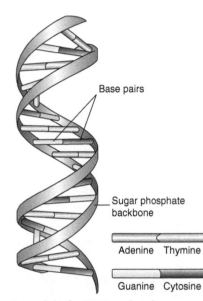

Base pairs

Sugar phosphate backbone

Adenine   Thymine

Guanine   Cytosine

A model of a DNA molecule

```
ATGCGTGCAATGTTTACGCGTAAAGCGTGCACGTTAGAGTACGTGCAGT
|||||||||||||||||||||||||||||||||||||||||||||||||
TACGCACGTTACAAATGCTCATTTCGCACGTGCAAGCTCATGCACGTCA
```

The order in which the bases are present in the DNA form a code that determines genetic information unique in each of us. Like notes on a piece of music form a melody, the nitrogen bases A, C, G, and T form the foundation of genetic properties. Despite the fact that there are only four bases, the possible combinations of even a hundred of these base pairs of DNA are enormous. And when considering the fact that the human DNA consists of 6 million base pairs, it is inevitable that DNA is unique for each person.

Previewing the Reading

Before you read about David Milgaard, read the following newspaper headlines related to him. They will help you understand who he is, and will build context for this chapter's reading.

a) Joining the ranks of the wrongfully convicted

b) Saskatoon police search for a killer

c) DNA test clears Milgaard

d) Justice Department orders review of Milgaard case

e) Larry Fisher convicted in murder of Gail Miller

f) Milgaard gets $10 million compensation package

g) No new trial for Milgaard

h) Who killed Gail Miller?

i) Police apprehend David Milgaard

j) Supreme Court orders a new trial

k) Milgaard leaves prison in legal limbo

l) A witness changes his story

First, try to put these headlines in sequential order (four of them have been done for you).

1. ____   4. _l_   7. ____   10. ____

2. ____   5. ____   8. _j_   11. _e_

3. ____   6. _g_   9. ____   12. ____

 Now, reread the headlines and try to build David Milgaard's story based only on this information. What kind of information is provided in the headlines? What do you think happened to him? To some degree you are practising a skill you studied in Chapter 6—making inferences.

Discuss and share your ideas about Milgaard's story with a partner.

ⓐ Science and Crime

Academic Word List (AWL) Vocabulary

The following AWL words will appear in this chapter's reading. Before completing the following exercise, skim the reading with a focus on the words in bold print. This will help you complete the table, and will prepare you for the reading.

implicate	empirical	entity	protocol
volume	subsequently	preliminary	component
specific	integral	credit	transmit
framework	file	income	distort
highlight	furthermore	vary	mechanism
goal	thereby	generate	underlying
nevertheless	infrastructure	evaluate	circumstances
phase	crucial	guarantee	comprehensive

Place each of the above AWL words under the appropriate heading. Use a dictionary if you need help.

Noun	Verb	Adjective	Noun & Verb	Adverb	Noun & Adjective

Science and Crime at a Glance...

1   Faith in the criminal justice system is based on a belief in its effectiveness as a **mechanism underlying** the principle of egalitarianism. Most developed countries operate within a judicial system that **guarantees** equality before the law, where everyone is afforded equal protection and enjoys the benefits of laws without persecution because of ethnicity, nationality, sex, age, race, religion, or physical or mental disability.

2   **Nevertheless**, despite these grand ideals, there have been a growing number of criminal cases that **highlight** issues of wrongful convictions. Wrongful convictions, which occur when individuals have been convicted and sentenced for an offence they did not commit, undermine two important features of the criminal justice system: effectiveness and fairness. Wrongful convictions are not new **entities**. Due to scientific advances, **specifically** in forensic science, courtrooms around the world are now dealing with, or have recently dealt with, issues of wrongful conviction. The following is one such story.

3   David Milgaard was adamant about his innocence. Throughout his lengthy prison term, Milgaard insisted that he was blameless in the January 1969 stabbing death of 20-year-old Gail Miller. Miller, a nursing assistant, was stabbed in the back, front, side, and neck a total of 12 times, before being left on a snowbank to die in the city of Saskatoon, Canada. Forensic evidence indicated that she was then raped after being murdered. Police found only a bloodstained kitchen paring knife and Miller's bloodstained purse in a garbage can nearby—neither of them with Milgaard's fingerprints on them.

4   Milgaard found himself out of fortune's favour. Along with two friends—Nichol John and Ron Wilson—he was driving from Regina, in southern Saskatchewan, through to Alberta, via Saskatoon.

5   Five months after Miller's death, Milgaard was charged with her murder. He was only 16 years old. On that fateful night, the trio stopped to pick up another friend, Albert Cadrain, who resided close to where Miller's body was found. Initially, Cadrain pointed blame in Milgaard's direction, **distorting** the facts of the event. About one month after the murder, Cadrain informed police officials that he recalled seeing Milgaard's clothing bloodstained the day Miller was stabbed. This **empirical** evidence was an **integral** part of the police investigation. Milgaard's friends, Wilson and John, also **implicated** him. On 31 January 1970, David Milgaard was convicted and sentenced to life in prison for a murder he never committed. Exactly one year later, the Saskatchewan Court of Appeal upheld his conviction. Almost 10 months after that, the Supreme Court of Canada turned down his appeal.

6   Milgaard spent the next 23 years in prison. During that time, he continued to proclaim his innocence. Milgaard was also refused parole—he had never apologized for his actions. It would have been a moot apology, as he still maintained his innocence. An apology would be an admittance of guilt, but with it he would have been granted parole. **Invariably**, he refused to offer one.

7   In November 1991, then–Justice Minister Kim Campbell, under the duress of years of public pressure initiated by Milgaard's mother Joyce, who believed in her son's innocence since the day he was arrested, asked the Supreme Court of Canada to review Milgaard's case. Almost five months later justice finally turned Milgaard's way. The Supreme Court ruled that Milgaard was convicted on suspect evidence and unreliable testimony. The court **thereby** granted Milgaard a new trial. **Subsequently**, he was released after spending 23 years in prison, but he was not formally acquitted of his crime.

8   Five years later, DNA evidence proved Milgaard's innocence, and he was acquitted of the murder charges. In 1999, the Saskatchewan government apologized publicly to Milgaard and paid him $10 million in lieu of missed **income** and as an act of apology for taking away more than half his life.

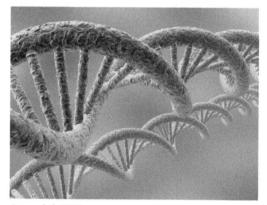

A model DNA structure

9   Milgaard's freedom rests largely upon DNA, the fundamental building block for an individual's genetic makeup. It is a **crucial component** of every cell in the human body. DNA is a powerful investigative tool used to convict suspects, and more recently, to exonerate those innocent individuals who were wrongfully convicted.

10   DNA **transmitted** from an individual's saliva, blood, semen, skin tissue, hair, and fingerprints that are found at a crime scene can be used to **generate** evidence in a trial. Many countries have adapted some form of DNA legislation, allowing the results of DNA testing to be used in the court of law. These laws often provide the legal **framework** for regulating the storage and collection of DNA. If used properly and not contaminated or tampered with, DNA, in many ways, can help those wrongfully convicted to get their convictions overturned.

11   Soon after Milgaard's acquittal, Larry Fisher, a convicted rapist and resident of Saskatoon, was found guilty of the rape and stabbing death of Gail Miller. The same DNA evidence that had set Milgaard free proved Fisher guilty. On 20 February 2004, a commission was set up to look into the wrongful conviction of David Milgaard. Not only was the commission examining Miller's killing and Milgaard's conviction, it also wanted to determine if the investigation should have been reopened before 1991, based on earlier information received by police officials. The commission's **goal** was to investigate what happened and to develop a **protocol** to help ensure this kind of thing does not happen again.

12   The inquiry cost $10 million and lasted a year. It was divided into four **phases**:

1. The preliminary investigation into Gail Miller's murder and David Milgaard's trial.
2. A look at information that came out after Milgaard's conviction and how the case was reopened.
3. Whether the investigation should have been reopened when police and justice officials received new information.
4. How the judicial infrastructure permitted the false conviction of Milgaard.

13   Almost two years after the end of the inquiry, the commission released its findings. It found that in 1980 police officials were in possession of information that could have pointed to Larry Fisher 12 years earlier than Milgaard's release date. The report stated that the information "might have led to Fisher as a serious suspect in 1980 had it been followed up." Instead, the report was "received, **filed**, referred and possibly **evaluated** on a cursory basis within the Saskatoon police, but it went no further. It should have," the report noted. "The criminal justice system failed David Milgaard," the commission concluded.

14   **Furthermore**, the 815-page report, released in two **volumes**, provided a **comprehensive** review of the Milgaard case, from the **circumstances** surrounding Miller's death to Milgaard's conviction, and even **crediting** the "epic struggle" led by Joyce Milgaard, who always believed in her son's innocence.

15   Milgaard's story has been depicted in various movies and is the subject of a 1992 song by the Canadian band The Tragically Hip.

Fill in the table below with three words from this article that are *not* from the AWL, but that are new for you.

Word	Part of Speech	Definition	Sample Sentence

Share your table with a partner.

Reading for Details

The following statements are incorrect. Correct them on the lines below.

1. Wrongful convictions are something new within the judicial system.

2. Fingerprints on the knife and Miller's purse helped identify Milgaard as the murderer.

3. Despite Wilson's and John's support, Milgaard was sentenced to life in prison.

4. DNA is only found in specific cells or specific parts of the body.

5. The 2004 report into the Milgaard case found that the criminal justice system did everything it could given the circumstances in which it found itself.

Discussion Questions

◎ Discuss the following questions with a partner.

1. Reread paragraph 5. What does *parole* mean? If you were Milgaard, would you have done the same thing even if it meant giving up your parole? Why or why not?
2. Milgaard was awarded $10 million by the Saskatchewan government for his troubles. Was this enough to compensate for 23 years of prison time? If not, how much would be enough? Do you think you can put a dollar value on something like this?
3. Excluding the use of DNA testing, what other steps do you think judicial systems can take to further prevent wrongful convictions? Make a list of three or four steps and discuss how they would work.
4. Imagine that you are a judge, and you are presented with the list you discussed in question 3 above. What problems are there with these steps, or what might some of the difficulties be in implementing these steps? (Be critical of your own ideas here!)

Vocabulary Practice

Definitions

Match the words below with their appropriate definitions.

Words	Definitions
1. nevertheless	_____ despite something that you have just mentioned
2. crucial	_____ one of several parts of which something is made
3. empirical	_____ a system of fixed rules and formal behaviour
4. subsequently	_____ used to introduce the result of the action or situation mentioned
5. furthermore	_____ extremely important, because it will affect other things
6. entity	_____ afterwards; later; after something else has happened
7. thereby	_____ based on experiments or experience rather than ideas or theories
8. integral	_____ being an essential part of something; having all the parts that are necessary for something to be complete
9. protocol	_____ in addition to what has just been stated
10. component	_____ something that exists separately from other things and has its own identity

Definitions taken or adapted from *Oxford Advanced Learner's Dictionary 8th Edition* by A. S. Hornby © Oxford University Press 2010. Reproduced by permission.

◎ Expanding Lexical Concepts

Collocations

Use the AWL vocabulary in the text box to form high-frequency collocations with thefollowing words.

income	highlight	framework
comprehensive	circumstance	goal
preliminary	mechanism	

1. basic, general, wider, existing, flexible, coherent, conceptual, theoretical, legal, historical, establish / set up / provide / within a _____

2. immediate, short-term, long-term, ultimate, main, primary, clear, explicit, specific, modest, achievable, attainable, realistic, elusive, personal, common _____

3. _____ list, exam, test, study, insurance, coverage, history

4. favourable, adverse, difficult, tragic, trying, unfavourable, exceptional, unusual, mysterious, unforeseen _____

5. personal, recorded, serve to _____; _____ of the day, week, year, etc.

6. firing, locking, steering, trigger, winding, effective, precise, underlying, complex, social, provide a
_____

7. _____ report, hearing, talks, investigation, expenses, round

8. steady, household, personal, extra, loss of _____; _____ tax, statement

Using Collocations

Fill in the blanks using the AWL word in parentheses with the correct collocation from the list on page 136. More than one answer may be suitable at times.

1. The number of alcohol sales to minors _____ problems with enforcing laws specifically related to youth. (highlight)

2. The accident occurred when the _____ locked, preventing the driver from avoiding oncoming traffic. (mechanism)

3. A _____ of mine is to lose five kilograms by Father's Day. (goal)

4. _____ coverage is recommended for travellers heading to high-risk countries. (comprehensive)

5. Part of her job description is to _____ upon which others can freely exchange their ideas. (framework)

6. A _____ is usually required in order to secure a bank loan. (income)

7. Whether it is a highly predictable situation, or an _____ police officers need to be prepared for anything. (circumstance)

8. The _____ suggested that Harris was not involved in the crime. (preliminary)

Word Forms

Fill in the blanks with the appropriate form of the AWL vocabulary.

1. The theme which _____ the entire first chapter is one of heartbreak and sorrow.
   a) underlay   b) underlies   c) underlie   d) underlying

2. The diverse _____ presented at the conference highlight the importance of cost-cutting procedures in any environment.
   a) variance   b) variability   c) varies   d) variables

3. Her brother was _____ in the murder trial of his girlfriend.
   a) implication   b) implicating   c) implications   d) implicated

4. The hydroelectric project was designed to _____ enough power to support a community of 50,000 people.
   a) generate   b) generating   c) generated   d) generates

5. Establishing a secure line of _____ is looked upon highly by various financial institutions.
   a) creditors   b) credits   c) creditor   d) credit

6. Student _____ can sometimes help instructors improve their teaching methodology.
   a) evaluation   b) re-evaluations   c) evaluations   d) evaluates

7. _____ lines are sometimes responsible for moving energy from one location to another.
   a) Transmission   b) Transmit   c) Transmitted   d) Transmitting

8. Some guitarists use a _____ pedal to alter the sound the guitar produces.
   a) distorting   b) distortion   c) distorts   d) distorted

9. The police officer replied: "Without going into _____, let's just say we're aware of the circumstances involved with the attempted robbery."
   a) specific   b) specifications   c) specifics   d) specificity

10. When asked which _____ he was about to begin, the surgeon replied with a blank stare.
    a) phases   b) phasing   c) phase   d) phased

Before Moving On...

About Rock and Roll

Rock and roll was discussed earlier in Chapter 4. What do you remember about it? Answer the following questions with a partner:

1. When and from where did rock and roll emerge?

2. What musical genres influenced the birth of the rock and roll sound?

3. Rock and roll grew out of a desire to express what differently at the time of its birth?

4. Who are some of the early musicians or bands that helped shape rock and roll?

♫ A Science-and-Crime Song: "Wheat Kings"

About the Artists

The Tragically Hip is a Canadian rock band that formed in Kingston, Ontario, in 1983. It wasn't until 1989 that they produced their first studio album, and by the mid-1990s they were selling out concerts across Canada and the American Midwest. Led by vocalist Gordon Downie, The Hip (as they became known) grew famous for their commanding and energetic stage presence, and for their ability to produce a live, tight sound on stage that few bands can match. At times they manage to ride a fine line between indie and alternative rock and rock, drawing on fans from both genres. As a result The Hip continues to sell out shows across North America. They are still producing music and playing live shows today.

Listen to the song and try to fill in the blanks. You will have two opportunities to hear the song.

The Tragically Hip—"Wheat Kings"

Sundown in the Paris of the prairies*
Wheat kings have all their _____ _____
And all you hear are the _____ _____
Pushing around the weather vane* Jesus.

In his Zippo lighter, he sees the killer's face   5
Maybe it's someone standing in a killer's place
_____ _____ _____ _____, well that's nothing new,
besides, no one's interested in something you didn't do
Wheat kings and pretty things,
let's just see what the morning brings.   10

There's a dream he dreams where the high school is dead and stark
It's a museum and we're all locked up in it after dark
The walls are lined all yellow, _____ _____ _____
Hung with pictures of our parents' prime ministers
Wheat kings and pretty things,   15
wait and see _____ _____ _____.

Late-breaking story on the CBC*,
A nation whispers, "We always knew that he'd go free"
They add, "You can't be _____ of living in the past,
'cause if you are _____ _____ _____ _____ _____ you're gonna last." 20
Wheat kings and pretty things
let's just see what tomorrow brings
Wheat kings and pretty things,
that's what tomorrow brings.

*Song Vocabulary

prairie (noun): a wide flat area of land in North America, without many trees and originally covered
with grass
vane (noun): a flat blade that is moved by wind or water and is part of the machinery in a windmill,
etc.
CBC (noun): the Canadian Broadcasting Corporation (a national organization that broadcasts
television and radio programs)

Definitions for *prairie* and *vane* taken from *Oxford Advanced Learner's Dictionary 8th Edition* by A. S. Hornby. © Oxford University
Press 2010. Reproduced by permission.

Listen Again!

Listen to the song again and double-check your answers. When you are finished, check your answers
with a partner.

Song Survey

In the last column provide a reason for your choice.

1. Were the lyrics easy to understand?	Yes	No	
2. Do you feel this song is typical of rock music?	Yes	No	

3. Would you listen to more songs by The Tragically Hip?	Yes	No	
4. Is this the kind of song your parents would listen to?	Yes	No	
5. Would you recommend this song to your friends?	Yes	No	

Share your answers with a partner.

◎ Song Discussion

Discuss the following questions in small groups.

1. What might the phrase *wheat kings* be a metaphor for?
2. Reread lines 19–20. What do you think the message of The Tragically Hip is here? Have you ever "lived in the past"? If so, explain the situation.
3. Study the lyrics to this song and identify two literary devices (refer back to pages 16–17, where literary devices were first introduced if you need help). Then explain the effect these literary devices have on the song as a whole.

Focus on Reading

Skills Focus: Reading for Arguments and Counter-Arguments

Texts often present both sides of an argument. This is done for numerous reasons: to project a balanced opinion; to present a critical analysis of material; or to entertain objections to the idea being promoted. Whatever the reason, being able to quickly identify these arguments will help you understand the main points of a reading, and more importantly, allow you to make an informed decision based on multiple perspectives.

Skills in Practice

In the reading below, adapted from the *New York Times*, the author presents various pieces of information regarding the murder trial of Rubin "Hurricane" Carter. Like Milgaard, he too was sentenced to life in prison for a crime he did not commit. As you are reading highlight the arguments and counter-arguments that are presented by the author. (You will, of course, first have to identify the purpose of the reading and understand the context in which the facts are presented.)

Hurricane Carter Case is Back in Court

After 20 years of trials, retrials and reversals, the case of Rubin (Hurricane) Carter is back in court.

Last week, a Federal appeals court in Philadelphia began reviewing prosecution and defense briefs on whether to reinstate Mr. Carter's conviction for murder in the fatal shootings of three people in a bar in Paterson, N.J., in 1966.

Mr. Carter was released from a New Jersey prison in November 1985, after his second conviction had been overturned by a Federal judge in Newark. Once outspoken and lionized as a civil-rights cause célèbre, the 49-year-old former contender for the middleweight boxing title now leads a secluded life, refusing to be interviewed or disclose where he is living.

In an uncharacteristic strategy for prosecutors, the Passaic County Prosecutor's office said in its appeals brief that the Federal judge, H. Lee Sarokin, had "slanted and **distorted** views of the case" and had created a "terrible injustice" by freeing Mr. Carter and his co-defendant, John Artis.

Results of Lie Detector

Judge Sarokin ruled that the prosecution at a 1976 trial had violated the constitutional rights of Mr. Carter and Mr. Artis through a racially biased summation in which he said that the defendants, who are black, fatally shot three whites for racial revenge in the bar. Judge Sarokin also found that the prosecution had misrepresented evidence about the results of a lie-detector test that could have impeached the sole witness who had placed Mr. Carter and Mr. Artis at the murder scene.

Defense lawyers, in a brief submitted last week, said the prosecutors had made gratuitous attacks on Judge Sarokin on the theory that if they had repeatedly said Mr. Carter and Mr. Artis "'really did it,' then serious constitutional errors will be overlooked."

No date has been set for oral arguments before a three-judge panel of the appeals court. Mr. Carter's current silence is in marked contrast to his posture in 1976, when his first conviction on the murder charge was reversed.

Song by Dylan

While awaiting retrial, entertainers, politicians, executives, sports figures and civil-rights leaders courted Mr. Carter. Bob Dylan wrote a song about his struggle. In 1983, seven years after his second conviction, Mr. Carter said in an interview that he had been abandoned by most of his former supporters. "He is keeping very private and he has dedicated himself to reviewing the record and helping in the preparation of the briefs," Mr. Carter's chief lawyer, Myron Beldock, said. A friend of Mr. Carter, Fred Hogan, an investigator for the New Jersey Public Defender's office, said Mr. Carter was staying with relatives in New Jersey. "He realizes there is nothing to gain by getting involved in a media hype," Mr. Hogan said.

Mr. Carter, who had been sentenced to a minimum term of 30 years in prison, had served almost 19 years before his release in 1985.

The tangled Carter-Artis murder case began with the fatal shootings of two men and a woman in the Lafayette Bar and Grill in the early hours of June 17, 1966. Three months later, Mr. Carter, then 30 and a boxer who had fought for the middleweight championship, and Mr. Artis, then 20, were indicted in the slayings. Both were convicted in a jury trial in May 1967.

The case was reopened in 1974, after two prosecution witnesses recanted their identifications of Mr. Carter and Mr. Artis as the gunmen. Both witnesses said they had been pressured by detectives to give false testimony at the trial.

Contentions in Appeal

In March 1976, the New Jersey Supreme Court overturned the first conviction on the ground that evidence about leniency and other favors offered the two prosecution witnesses had been suppressed. Nine months later, however, a jury convicted Mr. Carter and Mr. Artis, for a second time. The prosecution, in its appeal to restore the murder convictions, made these contentions:

- Prosecutors had legal grounds to cite a motive of racial revenge for the slayings of white people in a bar, because of a slaying earlier that evening of a black bar owner who was the stepfather of a friend of Mr. Carter.
- Mr. Carter and Mr. Artis were stopped shortly after the murders in a car that, two witnesses said, was identical to the getaway car used by the killers. Moreover, a shotgun shell and bullet found in the car were similar to ammunition used in the slayings.
- No evidence favorable to the defense was withheld about the lie-detector test, given to Alfred P. Bello, the sole witness who placed Mr. Carter and Mr. Artis at the crime scene.
- Three witnesses who provided alibis for Mr. Carter in 1967 testified at the second trial that they had lied at the first trial to help Mr. Carter.

Rebuttal by Defense

The brief by the Acting Prosecutor, John P. Goceljak, and his chief assistant, Ronald G. Marmo, emphasized that the State Supreme Court had upheld the convictions, four to three. In rebuttal, the defense brief made these contentions:

- The prosecution withheld the results of the lie-detector test that would have proved Mr. Bello was lying when he identified Mr. Carter and Mr. Artis.
- Mr. Carter and Mr. Artis did not fit witnesses' descriptions of the gunmen.
- Witnesses disagreed as to whether Mr. Carter's car resembled the one used by the gunmen. And the ammunition found in the car may have been planted by the police, because the rounds were not logged with the property clerk until five days after the murders.

◎ When you are finished, compare what you have highlighted with a partner, and then discuss the answer to the following question: Based on the information in this reading, do you believe that Rubin "Hurricane" Carter is innocent of the murder charges, or guilty? Provide evidence from the reading to support your answer.

Focus on Writing

Skills Focus: Writing a Compare-and-Contrast Essay

The compare-and-contrast essay is a popular style of essay writing often assigned by instructors. In this style of essay you are asked to identify the similarities and / or differences between two (usually) or more ideas. Instructors often favour this essay style because it requires you to analyze multiple perspectives on any given topic, to think critically about them, to synthesize them, and to go beyond just simple summaries—you need to provide an interesting analysis of the material in question that is relevant to the essay question or topic.

What kind of topics might you be asked to compare and contrast? With a partner create a list of four or five compare-and-contrast essay topics.

Brainstorming

Preparing to write a compare-and-contrast essay may be easier with the help of a Venn diagram. A Venn diagram will help you to quickly and efficiently compare and contrast two or more things or ideas.

In the central area where the circles overlap, list the traits the two items you are comparing have in common. In each of the areas on the extreme right and left that do not overlap, list the traits that are different.

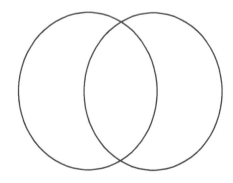

A Venn diagram

Finding a Focus

Once your Venn diagram has allowed you to collect a large amount of contrasting and similar points, the following will help guide you through deciding what to focus on in your compare-and-contrast essay:

- What's relevant to the course? (Is this a history course? a psychology course?)
- What's relevant to the assignment? (Read the essay question again)

- What's interesting and informative?
- What matters to the argument you are going to make? (What's relevant to my thesis statement?)
- What's basic or central (and needs to be mentioned even if obvious)?
- Overall, what's more important: the similarities or the differences?

Organizing Your Paper

Traditionally, there are two popular forms for organizing a compare-and-contrast essay: block style and point by point. Let's suppose, for example, that you are discussing the differences and similarities between the English and Australian legal systems. Further, after creating a Venn diagram, you have decided to discuss the following four points: courtroom time efficiency, lawyer fees, percentage of criminal convictions, and average length of sentence. Examine the following two diagrams. They outline how a compare-and-contrast essay on the English and Australian legal systems could be approached using either essay style.

Block Style

Introduction
(Thesis Statement)

⇩

England
courtroom time efficiency
lawyer fees
percentage of criminal convictions
average length of sentence

⇩

Australia
courtroom time efficiency
lawyer fees
percentage of criminal convictions
average length of sentence

⇩

Tie your main points or ideas together

⇩

Conclusion

The block model deals with each item of comparison separately, in one large block (which can be divided into numerous paragraphs). It provides for a body paragraph (or multiple body paragraphs) that brings together the main comparisons and/or similarities you have made. There is, however, one risk you should be careful of with this essay style. A block-style essay risks that you just write a list of points (something your instructor does not want). As the points you are making (the contrasts and similarities) are further away from each other on the page, identifying their relevance to the paper as a whole may prove difficult. Be sure that you do not just list points if you choose to use this essay style. And remember that each point should be connected to your thesis statement.

Point by Point

Introduction
(Thesis Statement)

⇩

England and Australia
courtroom time efficiency

⇩

England and Australia
lawyer fees

⇩

England and Australia
percentage of criminal convictions

⇩

England and Australia
average length of sentence

⇩

Conclusion

Instructors often prefer that you write using this format. This allows you to make your comparisons more directly, and allows for your ideas to come across more clearly. Note too that if you are arguing for a particular point of view (say, that overall, the Australian legal system is more efficient), then you should conclude each paragraph with a point that states such. This will reinforce your thesis and remind your reader of the point of your essay.

Transitions

Transitions also play an important role in a compare-and-contrast essay. They will help keep your readers focused on where you are in your paper (because you will be comparing and contrasting, you will be frequently shifting from one object of comparison to another, and this can be confusing). Here is a list of helpful transitions you should use in your writing, organized by comparison and contrast:

Comparison	
also	again
too	in addition
as well as	both
in the same manner	similarly
furthermore	like
moreover	not only… but also
	share the same

Contrast	
however	in contrast
unlike	in spite of
yet / but	conversely
on the contrary	nevertheless
instead of	although
even if	while
whereas	either… or

Skills in Practice

In 1967, the American boxer noted earlier, Rubin "Hurricane" Carter, was sentenced to life in prison for murder. In addition to the adapted *New York Times* article on pages 140–2, research the events surrounding his case. What are the similarities to David Milgaard's case? What are the differences? Follow the steps for composing a compare-and-contrast essay, and answer the following essay question: *Which of the two individuals named above suffered more injustice under the judicial system?* In your response be sure to identify either the similarities or differences in their situations.

As well as focusing on the compare-and-contrast aspect of the essay, be sure to keep in mind all of the writing skills you have been practising in the first seven chapters of this book. Take some time to review the writing sections of each chapter. This will help you produce a much higher-quality essay.

Focus on Listening

Skills Focus: Following a Linear Argument

A large amount of time in academics is spent defending a certain point of view. Many of your essays follow this format (defending your thesis statement), as do many of the research papers and articles that you will read on any given issue. Argumentation is a common form of communication people use to express themselves, either by spoken word, in written form, or even in film, music, and art. As you have already begun to notice (in your persuasive-essay writing, in your class debates, or even while discussing which basketball team is better with your friends) building a clear, strong argument requires practice.

Skills in Practice

Track 9: The Hardest Cases

One of the best ways to practise such argument building is to pay attention to professionals who do this for a living. Accordingly, you are going to listen to a 2011 report from an independent, non-profit news organization—ProPublica. The podcast is entitled "A.C. Thompson Details 'The Hardest Cases.'" This report deals with a poorly handled court case and its subsequent wrongful conviction. In this report, a journalist, A.C. Thompson, is interviewed. He outlines the criminal case of Ernie Lopez, someone who was wrongfully convicted for sexually assaulting an infant child.

In the program's introduction (the first 1:21), listen for the program's thesis, or its main point. What will this program try to demonstrate to you? Answer below in one or two sentences.

_____

_____

_____

Listen to the introduction again. How does the interviewer establish the context of the interview, and how does he establish the creditability of A.C. Thompson. (In other words, why should we trust what Thompson has to say?) Answer below in one or two sentences.

_____

_____

_____

As you listen to the rest of the program take notes that trace or outline the argument being presented. Pay special attention to key points such as dates, figures (numbers), events, or other key factors that Thompson stresses. In creating this outline, note how the interviewer first builds context for the listener, explaining the situation with background information. Then, note how Thompson builds a strong argument for the point being discussed by first, explaining the situation, second, by explaining some problematic issues, and finally, by outlining his own argument for Lopez's innocence. Many of the listening skills you have practised thus far will be useful to you here. As such, take a few minutes to review the listening skills from Chapters 1–5 before you listen to the program.

Pre-Listening Vocabulary

coroner (noun): an official whose job is to discover the cause of any sudden, violent, or suspicious death by holding an investigation

cardiac arrest (noun): an occasion when a person's heart stops temporarily or permanently

lethargic (adjective): not having any energy or enthusiasm for doing things

autopsy (noun): an official examination of a dead body by a doctor in order to discover the cause of death

clot (noun; verb): a lump that is formed when blood dries or becomes thicker, preventing it from flowing; to form thick lumps

Definitions taken or adapted from *Oxford Advanced Learner's Dictionary 8th Edition* by A. S. Hornby © Oxford University Press 2010. Reproduced by permission.

When you are finished spend some time reviewing your notes with a partner or small group.

Focus on Speaking

Skills Focus: Defending an Argument

Much like a persuasive essay, building an oral argument that is supported with facts is an important skill to master. (The piece you just listened to is an excellent example of this.) This will allow you to orally defend your ideas and to try and persuade others that your ideas are correct. An effective way to go about building your argument is similar to the way you build an argument with your essay: you need to decide what it is you wish to present or defend (what will you argue for or against), and then you will need to do research to uncover information that supports your position. You may want to structure your oral argument as follows:

1. Background information (establish some context)
2. State your intention (your thesis, or what you want to prove or argue)
3. Begin to provide evidence that supports your argument
4. End with a summary that also encourages your audience to act on your ideas ("Based on..., we should...." (You're inviting the listener to take action.)

As members of an audience, we can be persuaded from numerous perspectives. Two important elements of persuasion, listed in order of importance, include (from the Greek language): *logos* and *pathos.*

- Logos: The focus here is on the evidence you present in your argument. Is the evidence from a credible source? Is it logical? Is it arranged logically? Your evidence may come in various forms, including statistics, analogies, diagrams, or examples, depending on your situation.

- Pathos: The focus here is on how well you appeal to your audience's emotions. This tactic is popular in everyday communication. ("Are you *sure* you don't want to come with me?" appeals to a feeling of guilt at leaving the speaker alone.) People are often moved by their emotions.

The central focus of your argument should always be the logos, but it won't hurt you if you make some form of emotional appeal—just as long as your key arguments still focus on evidence and logic. You may want to add, for example, a rhetorical question (see page 6 for a review) to the end of a logical argument ("For these reasons advertising should be banned in elementary schools. Furthermore, would you want your seven-year-old son or daughter exposed to advertising while they should be studying?") Note that most instructors will *not* want you to include elements of pathos in your academic writing. In your writing you should rely almost exclusively on logos and good, clear writing skills.

Choosing the Right Words

Choosing which words to use can also help you influence an audience. Review the words below. They include words that are typical of defending or criticizing a position (note that although the words are divided into two lists, they can be used from either perspective—what is listed here is the more popular usage).

Defending someone or defending a position	Criticizing someone or criticizing a position
undeniable	lack of
phenomenal	failed to
certainty	weak
with certainty	impossible
quintessential	loose
unquestionable	questionable
worthwhile	suspicious
without fail / fault	open to interpretation
exceptional	inconclusive
necessary / necessity	rejection
	circumstance
	unreliable

◎ Skills in Practice

With the advent of DNA testing, wrongful convictions are frequently being overturned. Perform both Internet and print research on someone who was wrongfully convicted. Look into the details of their legal case, keeping the following assignment in mind:

Imagine that you are a reporter who believes in the innocence of the person you are researching, and imagine that your research is taking place two years before he or she was granted freedom (or the present day if he or she is still in prison). Present facts and evidence and build an argument or case that would help free this person from prison. Be sure to include the four points outlined on page 146. Also, use this chapter's listening exercise as an example for your own argument (although you do not have to present your argument in an interview format). As well as using the skills studied in this chapter, review those speaking skills studied on pages 90–91 and 127–8 to help you. Furthermore, be sure to include words from the lists above as well as AWL vocabulary words in your argument.

When your research is complete, prepare to present your argument to a small group or to your class. If you are listening, be prepared to ask the speaker questions when they are finished (review how to prepare questions while listening on pages 103–4). If you are the speaker, prepare to think on your feet (pages 30–32 for a review) in order to answer any questions you may receive during or after your presentation.

Additional Vocabulary

Word	Part of Speech	Definition	Sample Sentence

Space Exploration

Introduction

In April 2010, American president Barack Obama made the following remarks regarding space exploration: "By the mid-2030s, I believe we can send humans to orbit Mars and return them safely to Earth. And a landing on Mars will follow. And I expect to be around to see it." What kind of planning would be required to make this a success? With a partner outline five to eight steps that a country or space organization might have to do to achieve this immense goal.

Previewing the Reading

Track 10: Colonizing the Moon

Preview the upcoming reading by listening to a short commentary by the well-known science-fiction writer Isaac Asimov. In this piece, he discusses the possibility of colonizing the moon. Take notes while you are listening and summarize his comments.

When you are ready, discuss your summary with a partner. When you are finished, discuss the possibility of colonizing the moon. Do you think it is possible in the near or distant future? What kind of life could you have on the moon? How would you

A rendering of a Mars Rover explorer

grow food? What kind of entertainment would exist? Finally, Asimov sounds very confident. Why do you think he is so sure that humans will colonize the moon?

Space Exploration

Academic Word List (AWL) Vocabulary

The following AWL words will appear in this chapter's reading. Before completing the following exercise, skim the reading with a focus on the words in bold print. This will help you complete the table, and will prepare you for the reading.

administrate	evident	predict	accumulate
display	theory	image	require
project	document	priority	investigate
deny	finance	survive	series
ensure	create	structure	environment
method	media	demonstrate	author
consist	technology	objective	data
site	undertake	analyze	symbol
comment			

Place each of the vocabulary words under the appropriate heading below. Use a dictionary if you need help.

Verb	Noun	Noun & Verb	Adjective	Adjective & Noun

Space Exploration at a Glance...

1   The competition to land on the moon was a product of the Cold War. Not only was it an effort to prove **technological** superiority, but there was also a fear from the Soviet Union and the United States that either side might place weapons of mass destruction in space, although little **evidence** at the time supported these worries outside **media**-reported events.

2   The Soviet Union was ahead of the United States in this effort. So far, they had placed the first artificial satellite in orbit in 1957. In 1961, Soviet cosmonaut Yuri Gagarin became the first human to orbit Earth. From the time he entered office in 1961, US president John F. Kennedy made it a **priority** of his **administration** to place a man on the moon. The logistics of such an operation were immense, and the **project** was placed under the guidance of the National Aeronautics and Space **Administration** (NASA).

3   The early manned flights of the Mercury and Gemini missions **demonstrated** that humans could **survive** in space. The Apollo missions came next. Their purpose would be to land humans on the moon. However, this was a serious **undertaking**, and **required** a **series** of missions to space—more than 20 Apollo missions were planned. This was also a heavy **financial** burden on the US government.

4   Early in the program, a tragedy killed three astronauts and almost stopped the **project**. After an investigation had been completed, and changes made, the program continued. Following a **series** of unmanned space expeditions, the manned Apollo missions began with Apollo 7's Earth orbit. Apollo 9 was another Earth-orbit mission, and the Apollo 10 mission was a complete staging of the Apollo 11 mission without actually landing on the moon. NASA needed to **create** an **environment** where everything was **predictable** to **ensure** success. The space program needed consistent **data** and a **stable methodology** upon which to build their Apollo 11 mission plans and, with almost a dozen Apollo flights behind them, NASA was finally satisfied that they had **accumulated** enough information.

5   The Apollo 11 launch was set for 16 July 1969. The astronauts on board included Neil A. Armstrong, Michael Collins, and Edwin E. "Buzz" Aldrin Jr. The launch was a success. The first human journey to the surface of the moon began at Kennedy Space Center, Florida, with the liftoff of Apollo 11 aboard a Saturn V rocket booster **created** to bring the crew into space.

6   On 20 July 1969, after a four-day trip, the Apollo 11 astronauts arrived at the moon and the spacecraft was placed into lunar orbit. Buzz Aldrin carefully navigated his way to the lunar surface. He had to fly longer than planned, to avoid a field of boulders, and touched down at 4:18 PM with less than 40 seconds of fuel remaining. Upon landing, mission commander, Neil Armstrong spoke these now-famous words: "The Eagle has landed," a phrase that has since been borrowed by **authors** and movie directors alike.

7   It took six hours to prepare to exit the lunar module. At 10:56 PM EDT, Armstrong became the first human to set foot on the moon, marking the occasion with these words, "That's one small step for man, one giant leap for mankind." The Apollo lunar-surface camera, mounted on one of the legs of the module, **displayed** this event to the world, **documenting** it for all of humankind.

8   After arriving on the lunar surface, Armstrong and Aldrin detached a sheet of stainless steel to unveil a plaque that was read to the television audience: "Here men from the planet Earth first set foot upon the Moon, July 1969 A.D. We came in peace for all mankind."

9   Of the many experiments performed on this mission, one experiment actually used the footprints of Aldrin. The footprints left by the astronauts are more permanent than most solid structures on Earth. Barring a chance meteorite collision, these impressions in the lunar soil will probably last for millions of years. Photographs of the footprints were made so as to study the nature of lunar dust and the effects of pressure on the moon's surface. Twenty-one kilograms of lunar surface material was also collected for **analysis**.

10   One of the most iconic **images** of the last century was also **created** during this mission: the planting of the American flag on the lunar **site**. The rod to hold the flag out horizontally would not extend fully, so the flag ended up with a slight waviness, giving the appearance of being windblown. According to some **theorists**, the planting of the flag was an **undeniable** message to the Soviet Union that the US had won the space race.

11   There were five more trips to the moon, as well as the excitement of Apollo 13's near-disaster, culminating in the last man leaving the moon aboard Apollo 17 in 1972.

12   The day before Apollo 11 returned to Earth, Aldrin **commented**, "We feel this stands as a **symbol** of the insatiable curiosity of all mankind to explore the unknown." With the success of Apollo 11, the national **objective** originally put forward by President Kennedy, to land men on the moon and return them safely to Earth, had been accomplished.

Fill in the table below with three words from this article that are *not* from the AWL, but that are new for you.

Word	Part of Speech	Definition	Sample Sentence

Share your table with a partner.

Reading for Details

The following statements are incorrect. Correct them on the lines below.

1. The first man to walk in space was the Soviet cosmonaut Yuri Gagarin.

_____

2. The Apollo missions demonstrated to the world that humans could indeed survive in outer space.

_____

3. Apollo 11 was the name of the rocket that carried the astronauts to the moon.

_____

4. Similar to objects here on Earth, Buzz Aldrin's footprints are likely to last millions of years if left undisturbed.

_____

5. A slight breeze gave the American flag the appearance of being windblown.

_____

Discuss your answers with a partner. Try to use this chapter's vocabulary words as often as you can in your discussion.

Discussion Questions

◎ Discuss the following questions with a partner.

1. What is the importance of the Apollo 11 mission in relation to the Cold War? Think back to Chapter 1 where the Cold War was first introduced.
2. Try to see this event from the perspective of the Soviet Union. What might have been their reaction to America's success in outer space?
3. Apollo was an ancient Greek and Roman god associated with truth, prophecy, music, poetry, light, and the sun. Given this information, why do you think the name Apollo was given to this series of missions?
4. Aside from advancing technological capabilities, what other benefits do you think the United States obtained from this lunar landing?
5. Comment on Neil Armstrong's famous line when he stepped out onto the lunar surface for the first time, "That's one giant step for man, one giant leap for mankind." First, what does he mean by this? Second, what other historical events could be considered worthy of such an expression?

Vocabulary Practice

Definitions

Match the words below with their appropriate definitions.

1. finance 2. undertake 3. method 4. predict 5. accumulate 6. consist 7. document 8. display	_____ an official paper or book that gives information about something, or that can be used as evidence or proof of something; to record the details of something
	_____ money used to run a business, an activity, or a project; to provide money for a project
	_____ to gradually increase in number or quantity, or to get more and more of something over a period of time
	_____ to make yourself responsible for something; to agree or promise that you will do something
	_____ to have something as the main or only part or feature; to be formed from the things or people mentioned
	_____ a particular way of doing something
	_____ to say that something will happen in the future
	_____ to show something to people; an arrangement of things in a public place to inform or entertain people or advertise something for sale

Definitions taken or adapted from *Oxford Advanced Learner's Dictionary 8th Edition* by A. S. Hornby © Oxford University Press 2010. Reproduced by permission.

Expanding Lexical Concepts

Collocations

Use the AWL vocabulary in the text box to form high-frequency collocations with the words below.

structure	investigate	environment
objective	priority	symbol
theory	data	
image	evident	

1. seem, clearly, plainly, strongly, perfectly, increasingly, sufficiently _____
2. partial, general, coherent, unified, conflicting, abstract, literary _____
3. alien, friendly, pleasant, healthy, stimulating, favourable, uncertain, unstable, dangerous, competitive, hostile _____
4. remain, truly, purely, reasonably, primary, principle, overall, long-term, short-term, stated, common _____
5. high, low, main, major, number one, top, immediate, urgent _____
6. basic, complex, coherent, stable, internal, sentence, corporate _____
7. accurate, reliable, raw, empirical _____; _____ collection, entry, storage, analysis, processing, transfer
8. clear, dramatic, powerful, universal, traditional, religious _____
9. carefully, properly, thoroughly, further, ask / agree / promise / aim to _____
10. positive, negative, clean-cut, public, corporate, powerful, vivid, distorted _____

Using Collocations

Fill in the blanks using the AWL word in parentheses with the correct collocation from the list above. More than one answer may be suitable at times.

1. At present, scientists have developed only a _____ about the universe's origin. (theory)
2. The ability to perform _____ is essential for any student doing research. (data)
3. To remain _____ one must approach any situation with a blank slate. (objective)
4. The committee was_____ the outcome of decisions made years earlier. (investigate)
5. The advertising company's primary objective was to develop a positive _____ that represented the brand's ideals. (image)
6. Due to their remote location, residents are often given _____ when it comes to improving public services. (priority)
7. It may not _____ at first glance, but the demand for farmers in rural communities is on the rise. (evident)
8. Universities offer students of any background a _____ in which to develop critical thinking skills. (environment)
9. The human body is a _____ studied in-depth by medical students. (structure)
10. The dove is a _____ of peace. (symbol)

Word Forms

Fill in the blanks with the appropriate form of the AWL vocabulary.

1. The board of directors called upon their chief financial _____ to discuss fiscal concerns.
   a) analysis   b) analyzer   c) analyzers   d) analyst

2. Obtaining the proper _____ of eggs in many recipes is essential for proper baking.
   a) consisting   b) consistently   c) inconsistent   d) consistency

3. In order to _____ the events of that evening, the primary objective of the lawyer was to outline each event in detail.
   a) recreate   b) creation   c) create   d) recreating

4. Some branches of psychology are concerned with the _____ approach people have to simple, everyday tasks.
   a) methods   b) methodology   c) methodical   d) method

5. The faculty _____ ordered the student to withdraw from his studies because of plagiarism issues.
   a) administrate   b) administration   c) administratively   d) administrates

6. Sports _____ are well-known for their excessive use of superlatives.
   a) commenting   b) commentator   c) commentaries   d) commentators

7. A hypothesis is usually designed with a certain degree of _____ in mind.
   a) predictable   b) predictably   c) predictability   d) unpredictability

8. Stephen King has _____ dozens of books of fiction.
   a) authorship   b) author   c) authoring   d) authored

9. Despite favourable empirical data, regulators still _____ advertisers access to the student population.
   a) denied   b) denying   c) denies   d) deniable

10. _____ rates for people lost in any desert are considerably low.
    a) Survivor   b) Surviving   c) Survival   d) Survived

Before Moving On...
About Brit Pop

Brit pop is a form or subgenre of alternative rock. As the name suggests, it developed out of the United Kingdom, finding much of its inspiration from British pop rock sounds produced decades earlier. Its birth in the late 1980s and early 1990s was in reaction to the US grunge music scene of the same time period, which was topping British music charts. Although categorized under one heading, Brit pop bands explored various sounds. At one end of the spectrum were experimental bands such as Radiohead; at the other were bands such as Oasis who stuck to a more traditional rock sound. Among other characteristics, Brit pop stresses lyrical quality, simple chord progressions, and is heavily guitar-based. It is from the centre of this music scene that the Inspiral Carpets emerged.

A Space-Exploration Song: "Saturn 5"

About the Artists

Inspiral Carpets originated from Manchester, England, and reached the height of their fame in the late 1980s and early 1990s. This zenith paralleled the rise of the "Madchester" music scene, named after the popularity that bands from Manchester were enjoying at the time. (Other noteworthy bands that rose out of this scene include the Stone Roses, Happy Mondays, and the Charlatans.) The Inspiral Carpets are well known for producing a long line of successful singles rather than great albums. Having started out as a garage punk band, they evolved into an outfit recognized for their psychedelic keyboards and guitars. In the late 1990s the band broke up and members went on to pursue other musical interests.

Listen to the song and try to fill in the blanks. You will have two opportunities to hear the song.

Inspiral Carpets—"Saturn 5"

Lady, take a ride on a Zeke 64
Jerry wants to be a rocket
That's a _____ misconception*
Says we haven't seen anything yet
Laying down the _____ corpse* of   5
President 35
The lady crying by his side is
The _____ _____ _____ alive

Saturn 5
You really were the greatest sight   10
_____ _____ on a summer's day
Houston is calling me back to her

Lady, take a ride on a Zeke 64
Jerry wants to be a rocket
That's a _____ misconception*   15
It says we haven't seen anything yet
Laying down the _____ corpse of
President 35
The lady crying by his side is
The _____ _____ _____ alive   20
Saturn 5
You really were the greatest sight
_____ _____on a summer's day
Houston is calling me back to her
An eagle lands and _____ _____   25
Full of people raises its hands
All hail the men who will walk up in heaven today

Monochrome* TV
All the things you ever represented to me
Take me once more, _____ _____ _____ _____ again   30

Chapter 9 • Space Exploration

156

Saturn 5

You really were the greatest sight

_____ _____ on a summer's day

Houston is calling me back to her

Saturn 5   35

You really were the greatest sight

_____ _____on a summer's day

Houston is calling me back to her

*Song Vocabulary

misconception (noun): a belief or an idea that is not based on correct information

corpse (noun): a dead body, especially of a human

monochrome (adjective): using only black, white, and shades of grey, or different shades of only one colour

Definitions taken or adapted from *Oxford Advanced Learner's Dictionary 8th Edition* by A. S. Hornby © Oxford University Press 2010. Reproduced by permission.

Listen Again!

Listen to the song again and double-check your answers. When you are finished, check your answers with a partner.

Song Survey

In the last column provide a reason for your choice.

1. Were the lyrics easy to understand?	Yes	No	
2. Would you listen to more songs by Inspiral Carpets?	Yes	No	
3. Would you recommend this song to your friends?	Yes	No	
4. Is this the kind of song your parents would listen to?	Yes	No	
5. Do you know any other Brit pop bands? If yes, who?	Yes	No	

Share your answers with a partner.

Song Discussion

Discuss the following questions in small groups.

1. Listen to the first 20 seconds of this song again. Discuss what instruments are being used, when the band introduces them, and how they are layered. What kind of effect does this create for listeners?
2. Based on what you know so far about the lunar landing, who can you infer "President 35" is that is referred to in the song? What else do you know about this president (think back to Chapter 1)?
3. Do you think this event was important enough to inspire a song? Why or why not? Can you think of any other adventurous explorations that might deserve a song?

Focus on Speaking

Skills Focus Review: Thinking on Your Feet

With a partner review the eight tips for thinking on your feet successfully (discussed in Chapter 2). What important points can you recall? When you're finished discussing, return to pages 30–32 to review.

Skills in Practice

As mentioned earlier in the chapter, Apollo was an ancient Greek and Roman god. Research another god (or goddess) from Greek or Roman mythology. Discuss his or her importance to the Greek or Roman culture. Then, research his or her influence on modern-day culture—for example, does this god(ess) appear in literature or film, or are there cities named after the god(ess)? When you are finished your research prepare a short presentation. Remember to keep the AWL words from this and other chapters in mind.

After your presentation answer questions from your classmates and your instructor—get ready to think on your feet!

Focus on Listening

Skills Focus Review: Listening for Gist and Details

In Chapter 5, you focused on listening for gist and details from a lecture on South African history. Although the skill itself remains the same, learning how to use it in different situations is important. What do you remember about this skill? Discuss what you can recall with a partner, and then take a minute to review pages 88–89.

Skills in Practice

Track 11: Space

As the concluding line of the earlier reading mentions, the landing of a human on the moon was the result of a target set out in 1961 by US president John F. Kennedy. Listen to an excerpt from one of his speeches, and answer the following questions regarding gist:

1. What is the goal of this speech?
2. What are the main ideas presented in this speech?
3. Imagine that your friend is about 10 minutes late for this speech. Afterwards she asks you, "What did I miss? What did he say in the first 10 minutes?" Tell your friend the gist of the speech. Refer back to Chapter 1's study of summarizing key points (pages 14–15). The advice and phrases listed there will help you with this exercise. (Practise with a partner.)

Listen again. This time listen for details and answer the following questions. The following listening cues may help you with this.

Listening Cues

Pay attention to the following phrases that might signify something of importance, or a shift in the topic:

Let me begin with…

Next…

Furthermore…

In addition…

Therefore…

First…

Second… (etc.)

Finally…

Note also shifts in intonation, pauses, and stress on certain words. These may also indicate important information, as well as belief statements such as:

I think…

I believe…

I deem…

I consider…

I feel…

1. Who does President Kennedy suggest the Americans are racing against to get to the moon?
2. What are the four national goals the president sets out for his nation to achieve?

    a) _____

    b) _____

    c) _____

    d) _____

3. What kind of commitment does he ask of each person working in the space program?
4. Look back at question 3 on page 158. After you explained to your friend the gist of the speech she missed, she asks, "Right. Did he give any details about his plan?" How would you answer this question? Give your friend the details of the speech. (Practise with a partner.)

Focus on Reading

Skills Focus Review: Evaluating Sources of Information and Reading for Arguments and Counter-arguments

Evaluating Sources of Information

What significant information do you remember about this skill? Discuss with a partner, and then turn to pages 51–52 of Chapter 3 to review.

Skills in Practice

Exercise A

Read the article on the next page, note its source, and determine whether it is credible or not. Be prepared to give reasons for your choice.

Source: _____ Credibility (circle one): High   Medium   Low

Reading for Arguments and Counter-arguments

You studied this skill in the last chapter. Again, discuss its important points with a partner, and then turn to page 140 to review.

Exercise B

Identify, list below, and then discuss the arguments and counter-arguments that are presented in the following article.

Arguments   Counter-arguments

_____   _____
_____   _____
_____   _____
_____   _____

The landing of a man on the moon is an event that is not without controversy. Many people believe that the entire lunar landing was a fake—that it was created in a film studio in an isolated area of an Arizona desert. Read the following article regarding this.

Vocal Minority Insists It Was All Smoke and Mirrors

They walk among us, seemingly little different from you or me. Most of the time, you would never know of their true nature—except that occasionally, they feel compelled to speak up.

Take an example from Lens, this newspaper's photography blog. A recent feature, "Dateline: Space," displayed stunning NASA photographs, including the iconic photo of Neil Armstrong standing on the lunar surface.

The second comment on the feature stated flatly, "Man never got to the moon."

The author of the post, Nicolas Marino, went on to say, "I think media should stop publicizing something that was a complete sham once and for all and start documenting how they lied blatantly to the whole world."

Forty years after men first touched the lifeless dirt of the Moon, polling consistently suggests that some 6 percent of Americans believe the landings were faked. The series of landings, one of the greatest gambles of the human race, was an elaborate hoax developed to raise national pride, many among them insist.

They examine photos from the missions for signs of studio fakery, and claim to be able to tell that the American flag was waving in what was supposed to be the vacuum of space. They overstate the health risks of traveling through the radiation belts that girdle our planet; and they understate the technological prowess of the American space program.

And while there is no credible evidence to support such views, and the sheer unlikelihood of being able to pull off such an immense plot and keep it secret for four decades staggers the imagination, the deniers continue to amass accusations to this day.

"There are smart, normal people who buy into these conspiracy theories," said Philip Plait, an astronomer and author who counters the conspiracy theorists point by point and at excruciating length at his "Bad Astronomy" Website. He is one of many people who have joined the fight to affirm that the lunar landing happened.

Even though the so-called evidence from the conspiracists can clearly be proved wrong, Mr. Plait said, understanding the proof can require a working knowledge of history and photography and of science and its methodology.

Mr. Marino, the author of the post on the Lens blog, is a 31-year-old architect born in Argentina. In an e-mail interview, he said that the political corruption during the years of dictatorship in his country shaped his thinking: "I started to realize how political corruption operates and how it is the interests of a few in power that really governs our world."

As he traveled the world—he now lives and works in China—he picked up books contending that the landings were faked and saw documentaries, he said, which paint a dark portrait of political manipulation during the Nixon administration and somehow ties in the Vietnam War, the *Titanic* and the Tower of Babel before even getting to the supposed photographic evidence of lunar deception.

Mr. Sibrel, a documentary filmmaker who ardently claims the landing a fake, and who also sells his films online, has hounded Apollo astronauts with a Bible, insisting that they swear on camera they had walked on the Moon. He so annoyed Buzz Aldrin in 2002—ambushing him with his Bible and calling him "a coward, and a liar, and a thief"—that Mr. Aldrin punched Mr. Sibrel in the face. Law-enforcement officials refused to file charges against Mr. Aldrin, the second man on the Moon.

In an interview, Mr. Sibrel said that his efforts to prove that men never walked on the Moon has cost him dearly. "I have suffered only persecution and financial loss," he said. "I've lost visitation with my son. I've been expelled from churches. All because I believe the Moon landings are fraudulent."

Ted Goertzel, a professor of sociology at Rutgers University who has studied conspiracy theorists, said "there's a similar kind of logic behind all of these groups, I think." For the most part, he explained, "They don't undertake to prove that their view is true" so much as to "find flaws in what the other side is saying." And so, he said, argument is a matter of accumulation instead of persuasion. "They feel if they've got more facts than the other side, and that proves they're right."

Harrison Schmitt, the pilot of the lunar lander during the last Apollo mission and later a United States senator, said in an interview that the poor state of the nation's schools has had predictable results: "If people decide they're going to deny the facts of history and the facts of science and technology, there's not much you can do with them."

 # Focus on Writing

◎ Skills Focus: Dealing with a Counter-argument

Thus far the essays you have produced deal strictly with defending your thesis statement from one perspective—yours. However, in order to produce a high-quality piece of academic writing, you need to add one more section to your argumentative or persuasive essay: a counter-argument. The counter-argument demonstrates to your reader that you have thought about other perspectives and potential criticisms, objections, or problems with your own thesis statement. A counter-argument brings up any problematic issues, and then provides a solution for them. Here's a quick example:

> You've just finished arguing that the US government should increase funding for space exploration for reason X. **(Next comes the counter-argument)**. However, someone else may argue that reason X will cause other problems, like having less money to spend on education. **(Now you need to provide a rebuttal, or an explanation as to why this isn't really a problem)**. Initially, this may be the case, but the advances in science that are needed to improve space exploration will help scientists. This knowledge will eventually transfer into the classroom, encouraging new ideas and advances in technology that will benefit everyone. Indirectly, and in the long term, this is a good investment in education too.

By dealing with counter-arguments, then, you show that you have thought of potential problems with your ideas, and have shown how you would deal with these issues. This strengthens your argument considerably.

The counter-argument is often located just before the conclusion. For essays that require a more in-depth analysis, you may offer a counter-argument after every point you make.

Essay Structure

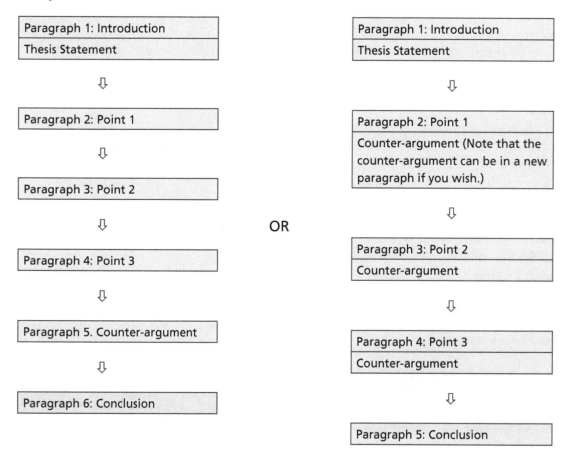

| Paragraph 1: Introduction |
| Thesis Statement |

⇩

| Paragraph 2: Point 1 |

⇩

| Paragraph 3: Point 2 |

⇩

| Paragraph 4: Point 3 |

⇩

| Paragraph 5. Counter-argument |

⇩

| Paragraph 6: Conclusion |

OR

| Paragraph 1: Introduction |
| Thesis Statement |

⇩

| Paragraph 2: Point 1 |
| Counter-argument (Note that the counter-argument can be in a new paragraph if you wish.) |

⇩

| Paragraph 3: Point 2 |
| Counter-argument |

⇩

| Paragraph 4: Point 3 |
| Counter-argument |

⇩

| Paragraph 5: Conclusion |

Skills in Practice

What did you think about the contents of the article on pages 160–1? Did a man really land on the moon on 20 July 1969, or did NASA falsify this event? Do some online and print research at your nearest library. First, evaluate your research according to what you studied in Chapter 3, pages 51–52 of this book. Second, write a short argumentative essay supporting your answer to the above question (again, see Chapter 3, page 52 to review argumentative / persuasive essays). Finally, be sure to include counter-arguments in your essay to strengthen your position (and don't forget to practise the relevant writing skills you have studied thus far in this book, especially the editing and proofreading stages of writing: pages 107–8).

Additional Vocabulary

Word	Part of Speech	Definition	Sample Sentence

Chapter 10

Elements of War

Introduction

Historians suggest that war has always been a part of human history. Wars have most certainly dated back to the beginning of recorded human history, and likely prior to that.

◎ With a partner, complete the following questions about war:

1. Why do you think war has been such a prominent part of human history? Discuss.

2. Together, make a list of five reasons why wars are fought.

Chariot warfare: Ancient Greece

3. Do you think war is a natural part of human evolution (i.e., that humans are naturally inclined to fight wars because of a constant lack of resources such as water, food, and oil; or a desire for more wealth, or power)? Defend your point of view.

LATUFF 2006

Previewing the Reading

◎ The topic of war often divides people. There are those who think it is a necessary evil, while others who suggest war does more harm than good. Preview this chapter's reading by taking a few minutes to study each of the following quotations. They represent various opinions on war and peace. Then, with a partner or in a small group, discuss the meaning and significance of each of these quotations.

"We make war that we may live in peace." —Aristotle, ancient Greek philosopher

"I find war detestable but those who praise it without participating in it even more so."
—Romain Rolland, writer

"When the power of love overcomes the love of power, the world will know peace."
—Jimi Hendrix, musician

"War has been more common than peace, and extended periods of peace have been rare in a world divided into multiple states." —Donald Kagan, historian

"Mankind must put an end to war, or war will put an end to mankind."
—John F. Kennedy, American president

"The object of war is not to die for your country but to make the other bastard die for his." —George S. Patton, US general

 # Elements of War

Academic Word List (AWL) Vocabulary

The following AWL words will appear in this chapter's reading. Before completing the exercise below, skim the reading with a focus on the words in bold print. This will help you complete the table below, and will prepare you for the reading.

domain	paradigm	construct	implicit
conflict	justify	correspond	ethical
similar	philosophical	mutual	relevant
evolve	external	conception	emphasize
initial	deviate	lecture	precede
adjust	phenomenon	assess	orientation
overseas	compound	coherence	

Place each of the above vocabulary words under the appropriate heading in the chart below. Use a dictionary if you need help.

Verb	Noun	Adjective	Noun & Verb	Noun, Adjective, & Verb	Adjective & Adverb

Elements of War at a Glance...

Defining War

1 War should be understood as an intentional and widespread armed **conflict** between political communities. Thus, a fight between individual persons does not count as a war, nor does a gang fight, nor does a large-scale family feud. War is a **phenomenon**, which occurs only between political communities, defined as those entities which either are states or intend to become states. Classical war **corresponds** with international war, a war between different states, like the two world wars. But just as frequent is war within a state between rival groups or communities, like **civil** wars. Certain political pressure groups, like terrorist organizations, might also be considered "political communities," in that they are associations of people with a political purpose and, indeed, many of them aspire to statehood or to influence the development of statehood in certain lands.

2 Having loosely defined war, then, we may go on to ask ourselves, is war **justifiable**? Answers to this kind of question fall under the **domain** of just-war theory.

Just-War Theory

3 Just-war theory deals with the **justification** of how and why wars are fought. The **justification** can be either theoretical or historical. The theoretical aspect concerns **ethically justifying** war and the forms that warfare may or may not take. The historical aspect, or the "just-war tradition," deals with the historical body of rules or agreements that have applied in various wars across the ages. For instance, international agreements such as the Geneva and Hague conventions are historical rules aimed at limiting certain kinds of warfare, but it is the role of **ethics** to examine these institutional agreements for their **philosophical coherence**, as well as to inquire into whether aspects of conventions ought to be changed.

A parody of just-war theory

4 Historically, the just-war tradition—a set of **mutually** agreed rules of combat—may be said to commonly **evolve** between two culturally **similar** enemies. That is, when values are shared between two warring peoples, we often find that they **implicitly** or explicitly agree upon limits to their warfare. But when enemies differ greatly because of different religious beliefs, race, or language, and as such they see each other as "less than human," war conventions are rarely, or unevenly, applied. It is only when the enemy is seen to be a people, sharing a moral identity with whom one will do business in the following peace, that tacit or explicit rules are formed for how wars should be fought.

5 Regardless of the **paradigms** that have historically formed, it has been the concern of the majority of just-war theorists that the lack of rules to war or any asymmetrical morality between enemies should be denounced, and that the rules of war should apply to all equally. That is, just-war theory should be universal, regardless of theoretical or historical perceptions.

The Role of Human Nature and War

6   A setting to explore the relationship between human nature and war is provided by the **philosopher** Thomas Hobbes. Hobbes is adamant that without an **external** power to impose laws, the state of nature would be one of immanent warfare. That is, "during the time men live without a common Power to keep them all in awe, they are in that condition which is called Warre; and such a warre, as is of every man, against every man," (*Leviathan*, 1.13). Many of the great **philosophers** who followed him, including John Locke and Jean-Jacques Rousseau, agree to some extent or other with his description. Locke rejects Hobbes's complete anarchic and total warlike state, but accepts that there will always be people who will take advantage of a lack of legislation and enforcement. **Initially**, Rousseau **deviates** from Hobbes. He inverts Hobbes's image to argue that in the state of nature man is naturally peaceful and not belligerent; however, when Rousseau elaborates on international politics, he is of a **similar** mind, arguing that states must be aggressive otherwise they decline; war is inevitable and any attempts at peaceful federations are futile.

7   Others reject the notion of an isolated individual pitted against others, prompting them to seek a contract between themselves for peace. These critics prefer an organic **conception** of the community in which the individual's ability to negotiate for peace (through a social contract) or to wage war is embedded in the social structures that form him. Reverting to John Donne's idea that "no man is an island" and to Aristotle's assertion that "man is a political animal," these proponents seek to **emphasize** the social connections that are endemic to human affairs, and, hence, any theoretical **construction** of human nature, and thus of war, requires an examination of the **relevant** society in which man lives.

8   Still others reject any theorizing on human nature. Kenneth Waltz, for example, argues that "[w]hile human nature no doubt plays a role in bringing about war, it cannot by itself explain both war and peace, except by the simple statement that sometimes he fights and sometimes he does not" (*Man, the State, and War*, 1954). The danger here is that this absolves any need to search for commonalties in warriors of different periods and **areas**, which could be of great benefit both to military historians and peace activists.

9   Much has been said thus far regarding the definition of war, how it can be **justified**, and the role human nature plays in war. But what effect does all of this have on the front lines of war? How does this affect the soldiers on the ground sacrificing their lives? The following describes the life of a Canadian soldier preparing to be deployed to Afghanistan.

A Soldier's Perspective

10   The last time I was on a military mission was 1994, when we were ordered to Rwanda. I was only 20, and it was my first **overseas** mission.

11   It's different this time. I'm nine years older, with a wife and two children. It's been an emotional rollercoaster as my family prepares for my mission to Afghanistan, and despite all the military preparation I keep dwelling on the unknown.

12   For my wife Nathalie, this will be her first tour as a military spouse. While I was at our military

compound attending **orientation lectures** and briefings that **precede** every mission, she was at home, preparing herself and our two children—ages six and four—for the experience. She has explained to them how Daddy won't be there for the first day of school, for birthdays and holidays. I feel like I am abandoning them.

13   We have tried to distance ourselves from each other, yet we remain close as the days fade away, in efforts to **adjust** to the **evolving** stress this is causing our family. While I hand over day-to-day tasks that once were mine, Nathalie assumes the burden of being married to a soldier. Managing the finances, the budget, and the shopping on her own will be a new experience and added stress.

14   We don't often discuss it, but we both know the realities of being a soldier and the spouse of a soldier. Our children are being raised to be aware of the world. They ask about the safety of Dad when he's in Afghanistan, why he needs to go, why he needs a gun if it's not dangerous, and what if he gets shot. These are questions boys that age shouldn't have to ask, but they come up every day. We try to soothe their fears, but their fears are real. We have been warned this deployment could be dangerous.

15   When it's time for me to go, we will hold each other, and say we'll be seeing each other soon. We won't say goodbye. I will board the bus for the trip to the airport and Nathalie will go home to our children. Then I'll be off on a mission I've been thoroughly trained for, but it feels like a voyage to the unknown.

The soldier's perspective is often forgotten about as newspapers **assess** the politics of war. The Arcade Fire song you will soon listen to has often been interpreted as aiming to bring the soldier's perspective into the spotlight.

Fill in the table below with three words from this article that are *not* from the AWL, but that are new for you.

Word	Part of Speech	Definition	Sample Sentence

Share your table with a partner.

Reading for Details

The following statements are incorrect. Correct them on the lines below.

1. Just-war theory primarily concerns itself with being able to identify and punish war criminals.

2. War between people of shared values often results in war that ignores previously established war conventions.

3. Hobbes argues that humans are naturally peaceful, but external powers urge them on to warfare.

4. Theorists who reject the idea of an isolated individual think understanding human nature and war requires that we understand each unique individual.

_____

5. The children of the soldier described at the end of the reading ask their father many questions because they are unaware of what is happening in the world.

_____

Discussion Questions

◎ Discuss the following questions with a partner.

1. Reread paragraph 5. Do you agree or disagree with the position of the just war theorists? Why or why not?
2. Do you agree with Rousseau's comment (paragraph 6) that countries need to be aggressive in order to be successful? Why or why not? Provide examples in your answer.
3. Outline the danger mentioned at the end of paragraph 8. Why do you think it might be dangerous? Explain in as much detail as possible.
4. Reread the first sentence of the third last paragraph of the reading. What might some of these unspoken realities be? Discuss in as much detail as possible.

Vocabulary Practice

Definitions

Match the words below with their appropriate definitions.

1. domain 2. implicit 3. phenomenon 4. overseas 5. mutual 6. paradigm 7. initial 8. deviate	_____ used to describe feelings that two or more people have for each other equally, or actions that affect two or more people equally; shared by two or more people
	_____ to be different from something; to do something in a different way from what is usual or expected
	_____ happening at the beginning; the first letter of a person's name; to mark or sign something with the first letter of your first and last name
	_____ suggested without being directly expressed; forming part of something
	_____ a typical example or pattern of something
	_____ connected with foreign countries, especially those separated from your country
	_____ an area of knowledge or activity; a set of websites on the Internet that end with the same group of letters, for example ".com," ".org"; lands owned or ruled by a particular person, government, etc., especially in the past
	_____ a fact or an event in nature or society, especially one that is not fully understood; a person or thing that is very successful or impressive

Definitions taken or adapted from *Oxford Advanced Learner's Dictionary 8th Edition* by A. S. Hornby © Oxford University Press 2010. Reproduced by permission.

Expanding Lexical Concepts

Collocations

Use the AWL vocabulary in the text box to form high-frequency collocations with the words below.

emphasize	assess	relevant
compound	adjust	coherence
conflict	lecture	

1. fully, accurately, properly, correctly, attempt / try / help / be difficult to _____
2. logical, achieve, create, maintain _____
3. bitter, violent, increasing, internal, regional, armed, political, social, religious, cause, come into, create, provoke, avert, prevent, end / settle a, a source of _____; _____ resolution, management, of interest
4. strongly, be important to, serve / tend / fail to, be at pains to, be keen to _____
5. slightly, gradually, rapidly, be difficult / hard to, need / take time to _____; _____ accordingly, for
6. seem, become, consider / deem sth, regard sth as, extremely, particularly, hardly, marginally, directly, no longer _____
7. fascinating, interesting, formal, impromptu, guest, public, course, severe, stern, deliver / give / attend / skip a, listen to a _____; _____ series, hall, room, notes
8. chemical, inorganic, organic, synthetic, dangerous, toxic, police, prison, military, walled in, secure, produce / form a _____

Using Collocations

Fill in the blanks using the AWL word in parentheses with the correct collocation from the list above. More than one answer may be suitable at times.

1. Salaries are often _____ every second year. (adjust)
2. The _____ housed a makeshift hospital, library, and post office for all members of the navy, regardless of their rank. (compound)
3. Any _____ the ongoing situation will result in insufficient results. (assess)
4. It's inevitable that he will fail the exam—he left his _____ on the bus. (lecture)
5. Logically structured essays _____ from start to finish. (coherence)
6. So much time had passed that the lawyers considered the documents _____. (relevant)
7. The minister dismissed herself from the meeting because of a _____; her brother was involved in the inquiry. (conflict)
8. Her report _____ and expand upon issues discussed in the original initiative. (emphasize)

Word Forms

Fill in the blanks with the appropriate form of the AWL vocabulary.

1. My aunt was in constant _____ with my uncle until his death.
   a) correspond   b) corresponding   c) correspondence   d) correspondingly

2. His response failed to provide any _____ for his malevolent actions.
   a) justification b) justifiable c) justifying d) unjustified

3. The judge's decision failed to set a satisfactory _____ for similar cases in the future.
   a) precedence b) precedent c) preceding d) precedes

4. It was difficult for the pilot of the lightweight aircraft to _____ himself in the heavy rain.
   a) orient b) orientated c) reorientation d) orientation

5. The investigation required a _____ of the crime scene.
   a) construct b) reconstruct c) constructive d) reconstruction

6. Many university philosophy departments offer the study of _____ as an option for its students.
   a) ethical b) ethically c) unethical d) ethics

7. Loosely defined, _____ biology focuses on the origin of species from a common ancestor.
   a) evolution b) evolutionary c) evolving d) evolved

8. A popular _____ axiom is that the same thing cannot both be and not be at the same time.
   a) philosophy b) philosophizing c) philosophical d) philosophized

Before Moving On...
About Indie Rock

Indie rock is by no means an easy genre to define. Musicians, critics, and fans alike have struggled to label it. Accordingly, the term itself remains ambiguous, as it readily adapts to the distinct sound that each new band creates for it. The term is used loosely to describe music that is produced "outside" the music industry (i.e., independent of big business music labels). Those involved in the music scene agree that it emerged as a genre out of both the United Kingdom and the United States in the early 1980s, gaining popularity in the 1990s with bands like Pavement, and more recently, The Killers, carrying with them commercial success that still resonates with many indie-rock bands today. Senior music writer for *Rolling Stone* magazine David Fricke went as far as to describe indie rock as "not a genre or a sound—it is a mission, a commitment to go your own way."

♫ An Elements-of-War Song: "Intervention"

About the Artists

Organized in 2003, Arcade Fire is an indie-rock band that formed in Montreal, Canada, around the husband and wife duo of Win Butler (vocals, guitar, piano) and Régine Chassagne (vocals, accordion, keyboards, hurdy-gurdy, drums).

Other band members include Richard Reed Parry (bass, guitar), William Butler (keyboards, guitar), Tim Kingsbury (bass), Sarah Neufeld (violin), and Jeremy Gara (drums). Their second album, in 2007, was recorded in an old Montreal church that the band had converted into a studio. Live shows by Arcade Fire include elaborate video montages and band members on various instruments—often giving the band an orchestra-like sound. Arcade Fire's latest album, *The Suburbs*, was awarded the 2010 Grammy Award for Album of the Year in the United States and the 2011 JUNO for Album of the Year in Canada.

A hurdy-gurdy

Listen to the song and try to fill in the blanks. You will have two opportunities to hear the song.

Arcade Fire—"Intervention"

The king's taken back the throne
The useless seed is sown
When they say they're _____ _____ _____ _____
I'll tell 'em you're not home

No place to hide   5
You were fighting as a _____ on their side
You're still a _____ in your mind
Though nothing's on the line

You say it's _____ that we _____
As if we're only mouths to feed   10
I know no matter what you say
There are _____ _____ you'll never pay

Working for the church
While your family dies
You take what they give you   15
And you keep it inside

_____ _____ _____ _____ _____ _____
Will die without a home
Hear the soldier groan*, "We'll go at it alone"

I can taste the fear   20
_____ _____ _____ and take me out of here
Don't wanna fight, don't wanna die
Just wanna hear you cry

Who's gonna throw the very first _____?
Oh! Who's gonna reset the _____?   25
Walking with your head in a _____
Wanna hear the soldier _____

Working for the church
While my family dies
Your little baby sister's   30
Gonna lose her mind

_____ _____ _____ _____ _____ _____

Will die without a home
Hear the soldier groan*, "We'll go at it alone"

_____ _____ _____ your fear   35
It's gonna lift you up and take you out of here
And the bone shall never heal
I care not if you _____

We can't find you now
But they're gonna get their money back _____   40
And when you finally disappear
We'll just say that you were never here

Been working for the church
While _____ _____ _____ _____
Singing hallelujah* with the fear in your heart   45
Every spark of friendship and love
Will die _____ _____ _____
Hear the soldier groan*, "We'll go at it alone"
Hear the soldier groan, "We'll go at it alone"

*Song Vocabulary

hallelujah (noun): a song or shout of praise to God

groan (verb): to make a long deep sound because you are annoyed, upset or in pain

Definitions taken or adapted from *Oxford Advanced Learner's Dictionary 8th Edition* by A. S. Hornby © Oxford University Press 2010. Reproduced by permission.

Listen Again!

Listen to the song again and double-check your answers. When you are finished, check your answers with a partner.

Song Survey

In the last column provide a reason for your choice.

1. Were the lyrics easy to understand?	Yes	No	
2. Would you recommend this song to your friends?	Yes	No	
3. Would you listen to more songs by Arcade Fire?	Yes	No	
4. Is this the kind of song your parents would listen to?	Yes	No	
5. Does this song inspire any emotions in you? If yes, which emotions?	Yes	No	

Share your answers with a partner.

Song Discussion

◎ Discuss the following questions in small groups.

1. Reread line 10. How might the meaning of this line change if the word *only* were removed? What might the significance of this word be here?

2. What literary device is used in both lines 24 and 25? What effect does this literary device create at this point in the song?

3. How might lines 17–19, 32–34, and 46–49 relate to a soldier's experience of war?

Focus on Writing

Skills Focus: Writing an In-Class Essay Exam

You may often be asked in university or college to write an in-class essay exam. In some ways, the same principles for writing a good out-of-class essay apply to writing a good in-class essay.

With a partner, discuss some key points that go into writing a good out-of-class essay that might also be useful when writing an in-class essay exam. Keep in mind what you've studied thus far, and make a list below.

1. _____
2. _____
3. _____
4. _____
5. _____

Despite these similarities, there are some key differences to keep in mind as you prepare to write an in-class essay exam. Likely, the most important of these is the purpose of your writing. Usually you write an out-of-class paper to learn more about a specific area of study; however, you write essay exams to demonstrate what you have learned. You are proving to your reader—your instructor—that you have mastered the study material and are comfortable with it. Your purpose for writing here is both informative and persuasive.

Below is some advice written by Emily Schiller, a former professor of Writing and American Literature at the University of California, Los Angeles (UCLA). It concerns how best to approach an in-class writing exam. Follow her advice closely, as the points she outlines will help you with your own exam writing skills.

Writing the In-Class Essay Exam

By Emily Schiller

The first in-class essay exam I took when I returned to college was a disaster. I had done all the reading, TWICE; thought extensively about the material; and filled pages with notes from my own responses as well as from class. I couldn't have been more prepared to discuss the novels we'd read.

But I wasn't at all prepared to write essays with time limits and no chance to revise. So what did I do? I took the questions as jumping-off points and wrote everything I could think of, had thought of, or might even consider. Every once in awhile I'd indent, so they at least would resemble essays with real paragraphs. There was no logic to anything I did; I just spewed. Not good. The professor commented (kindly, gently) that my ideas were superb and my insights quite inspired. However, not only were my answers not essays, they never really responded directly to the questions. Aargh!

After that, I learned to contain and direct my enthusiasms. Essay exams are not a license to babble. They require reflection and control. Here are some steps I created to help myself and, later on, to help my students.

1. First, read the question carefully. Pick out the salient points. What is the topic? A book, an event, an idea? What is the focus? A character? A problem? What are you being asked to do with this? Discuss? Contrast? Agree / Disagree?

2. Next, make a few very quick notes in answer to the question or in response to the topic.

3. Stop and take a breath. Read over your ideas and ask yourself which ones directly address the question or essay prompt. Throw out whatever is irrelevant to the task at hand no matter how much you love it. Really!

4. Now make a very brief (very rapid) outline:
   a) What is your thesis? What will you argue? Remember that your thesis is your promise to the reader: You are promising that by the end of this essay, you will have convinced the reader of such and such and nothing else. Once again, check to make sure the thesis responds directly and specifically to the question. The thesis will keep you honest as well as help prepare the reader.
   b) Create a list of the points you'll need to make to prove your thesis. Throw out any point that only shows off another bit of information you have in your head rather than builds the argument for your thesis. Each point should be in the form of an assertion, a mini-thesis and will serve as the topic-sentences for your body paragraphs.
   c) Arrange these topic sentences in some sort of logical order rather in the order they have just occurred to you. What piece of information does the reader need first? Second? etc. Each point should build on the one that comes before and towards making the case for your thesis.

5. Now start writing the essay. Do not let yourself write a long introduction. You don't want to take time away from the argument itself. Just use a sentence or two to introduce the problem being addressed, transition to your thesis, state your thesis, and then stop.

6. As you work your way through your body paragraphs—as specified in your brief outline— remember that each assertion needs an example as evidence. Your position means very little if you haven't demonstrated an ability to support it. That's what your professor is looking for. So specific, concrete evidence is crucial. If you are arguing that a character in a novel is greedy, don't simply assert that she is greedy. Give the reader an example from the plot that illustrates her nature and then explain or analyze how it does so.

7. Always try to leave yourself a few minutes at the end to look over your essays. They won't be perfect. No one expects that. But they should be clear, logical, and easy to read.

The steps I've outlined here aren't much different from the ones you'll use to write take-home essays, except that at home you'll have time to do lots of brainstorming and freewriting. In-class exams leave precious little time to be creative. But if you come to class prepared and then carefully tailor your insights to the questions being asked, you'll be able to express your ideas with grace and intelligence while staying on-topic.

◎ Skills in Practice

Below are two sample in-class essay exam questions related to readings from earlier in this book. On a separate sheet of paper, prepare to answer each essay question. Go through steps 1–4 outlined above. (Note that you do not actually have to write the essay—just practise the steps that will prepare you to write.)

1. Essay Question Related to Chapter 4:
   Identify and describe the causes leading up to the Bloody Sunday riots of 1972 in Northern Ireland.

2. Essay Question Related to Chapter 8:
   Explain, using examples, how DNA testing might be both beneficial and detrimental to modern society. Discuss too whether you support the use of DNA testing.

Skills Focus: Text Retention and Comprehension

Thus far you have studied various reading skills. When combined, these skills form the foundation for reading strategies that will help you more clearly understand and remember reading material. We will work through one such strategy in this last chapter. You should adapt this style to your own needs and continue to use it throughout your studies.

Survey-Question-Read-Recite-Review (SQ3R) Study Method

This technique suggests that you approach any study material using the following steps:

Survey

- Skim the reading to give you an overview of the material (obviously with longer texts or entire chapters of a book you will have to divide the material into chunks you find suitable).
- Note important titles or subheadings in the reading

Question

- Create questions from the article or chapter subheadings you noted above.
- These questions should give your reading purpose (the purpose being to get the answers to the questions you've formed).
- Use *who*, *what*, *when*, *where*, and *why* questions to guide you.

Read

- Read each section actively (i.e., find the answers to the questions you formed from the previous step).
- Pay attention to words in bold or those that are highlighted.
- If need be, underline or highlight important information, and ensure you study charts, graphs, and statistics.
- Read difficult sections more slowly; reread them if necessary.
- Read *only one section* at a time, and then move on to the next step.

Recite

- Talk to yourself. Orally ask yourself questions regarding the section you just read. Answering these questions (aloud) will give you a summary of what you just read.
- In the margins or in your notes, write down the answer to your questions or any other important ideas you remember; use your own words whenever you can.
- Reciting in this manner allows you to strengthen your learning: see (what you read), say (your oral summary), hear (your oral summary), and write (key notes and ideas). Together these form a strong foundation for reading comprehension.
- Repeat SQRR above with each section of the article or chapter you are reading.

Review

- Once you have completed the reading material, you'll have to review it. Look back at your questions and try to recall the answers and the main points under each heading. If you can't remember, glance back at your notes and the reading again. Once again, try to recall the main points, and then any sub-points (examples, statistics, etc.).

- Repetition. This should be done once or twice soon after the reading is completed (on the same day), and then periodically over the coming week(s) to maintain maximum retention and comprehension.
- Imagine writing an exam based on 10 chapters of a class textbook! You'll find this strategy *very* helpful when you're in this situation.

Skills in Practice

Return to this chapter's reading, and follow the SQ3R strategy outlined on page 177 to fill out the chart below.

War
Survey: Record important titles and subtitles from the reading.
Question: Write *who*, *what*, *when*, *where*, and *why* questions from main topics.
Read. Recite: Record key facts and phrases as needed for each question.
Review: Create a summary for each question. (This isn't always necessary but it will help.)

Skills Focus: Identifying Logical Fallacies

In Chapter 8, you looked at how to follow a linear argument, as well as how to defend one. Arguments, however, are often filled with errors in logic. For example, imagine that two people are arguing about music, and person A argues that Beethoven is the greatest composer of all time. Then imagine that person B replies with the following: "That's impossible. He wasn't very good. He was deaf for almost half of his life." There is a logical problem with person B's response. With a partner, try to work out what this problem is.

Logical fallacies are irrational arguments that are designed to change your opinion about a topic. They often appeal to emotions or psychological trickery in an effort to sway opinion in any persuasive argument. Below is a list of commonly used fallacies that you may come across on a daily basis (television news broadcasts, political debates, disagreements amongst classmates or friends).

1. Ad Hominem: an argument against a person or their character

   Example: "Basketball is better than baseball because many baseball players are overweight." (See also the Beethoven example, above.)

   _____

   _____

2. Straw Man: you create a similar, though different argument to the one that is being discussed, and this new argument is easier to criticize (however, this new argument was *not* the original argument—you've changed or simplified it in order to make it easier to defeat)

   Example: "The CEO wants to eliminate our factory's CO_2 emissions." "That's a bad idea. We won't be able to drive anymore, so no one will be able to get to work. We shouldn't support this idea."

   _____

   _____

3. Guilt by Association: the assumption that an idea (or person) must be wrong because it shares similar qualities with something (someone) else

   Example: "You enjoy using toothpaste X, but all children with teeth problems use toothpaste X. Therefore, you shouldn't use toothpaste X either."

   _____

   _____

4. Slippery Slope: arguing something is wrong because it is incorrectly assumed that negative consequences will follow

   Example: "Increased gun ownership will lead to an increase in the murder rate."

   _____

   _____

5. Non Sequitur: a conclusion or statement that does not logically follow from the previous argument or statement

   Example: "Seeing as fruit is good for your health, and with a lot of money you can buy a lot of fruit, a fruit farmer has the best job because he can get fruit for free."

   _____

   _____

6. Red Herring: the subject of the argument is changed (or irrelevant information is introduced as a distraction) in an effort to win the argument

    Example: "Kevin said that golf requires the greatest skill of any sport, but he didn't mention how much money baseball players make. Clearly, that makes baseball a better sport."

    _____

    _____

7. Improper Appeal to Authority: using a false authority to claim that your argument is correct

    Example: "My dad says that Shakespeare was the greatest writer ever."

    _____

    _____

An awareness of these fallacies is essential for two reasons:

1. awareness will help you find problems in other people's arguments (and prevent you from being deceived); and
2. awareness will help you avoid using them yourself.

Skills in Practice

1. Match the fallacy on the left with an example of it on the right.

a) ad hominem ____ b) straw man ____ c) guilt by association ____ d) slippery slope ____ e) non sequitur ____ f) red herring ____ g) improper appeal to authority ____	"If I pay for your sister to go to college, then I'll have to pay for you too, and then all of your friends as well—how ____ much money do you think I have?"
	"I can't believe the police stopped me for speeding. Thousands of children around the world died today because of malnutrition, and these cops are worried about my speeding. What I did was really not that worrisome. The police should be concerned about more important issues."
	____ "The judge, who had extra-marital affairs, is no position to make a decision regarding this murder trial."
	"My bicycle was stolen at the park, and Karen was at the park. Let's go and find Karen because she must have stolen ____ my bike."
	"Last year's Miss Universe claims that my skin cream is ____ superior to any brand you may have."
	"Most of Dave's friends have been to prison at least once. I don't think you should be hanging out with Dave."
	____ "We should review the laws regarding passport distribution." "No way! If we give out passports to everyone that comes here then we're going to have a ____ major immigration problem in this country."

2. Return to the examples of logical fallacies, starting on page 179, and write your own examples of each fallacy on the lines provided.

Track 12: Logical Fallacies

Listen to five arguments and identify the fallacy being used.

    i. _____   iv. _____

    ii. _____   v. _____

    iii. _____

Skills Focus: Applying Logical Fallacies

You will always be encouraged to avoid using logical fallacies in any argument. However, because of the frequency with which they occur, and the ease they create at seemingly defeating an opposing argument, people still frequently use fallacies (often unknowingly). One of the best ways to avoid using fallacies *and* to identify them is to actually practise with them. Think about it this way: it's hard to identify fallacy X that you are unfamiliar with, and it is even harder not to use fallacy X, when you don't even know what fallacy X is. In the exercise below you're asked to both use and avoid using fallacies in your arguments. In this manner, you will develop a much stronger understanding and awareness of their presence, thus allowing you to avoid using them in real-life situations.

Skills in Practice

Seven discussion topics are listed below. You should prepare a 30-second argument defending your point of view to a partner (refer back to pages 146–7 of Chapter 8 for how to prepare an argument). You will have to decide in advance with your partner if you will be for or against (column 2) the idea expressed in column 1. After listening to your partner's argument, in the last column identify if the argument is sound (✓) or not (✗). If it is not sound, identify the fallacy that was used to try and deceive you. While you are preparing for this, you should create *both* a logically sound argument (column 3), as well as a logically invalid argument (column 4). While you present your argument, you may choose to argue with a fallacy or not. (However, you should try to use a fallacy in at least four of the situations below. Remember, you and your partner are practising being able to identify a fallacy, which will be impossible if you don't use one.) Try to use this chapter's AWL words as frequently as possible in your arguments as well. The first one has been done for you.

Discussion Topic	Your Position (For or Against)	A Clear, Logical Argument	An Argument with a Fallacy	Fallacy Used	Your Partner's Argument (✓) or (✗)
1. Should teenagers be allowed to enlist in the military?	against	No, b/c research shows that brain of teens isn't developed like an adult's brain. Soldiers need to make serious, high-level cognitive decisions—something teen brains aren't ready for yet. So no teens in the military.	No b/c teens can't control large machines. My friend crashed his car; teens are going to crash tanks, too. Therefore, no teens in the military.	guilt by association	
2. Should companies be allowed to advertise to children?					

3. Do people have the right to own a gun?				
4. Should schools have standardized testing?				
5. Is the death penalty effective?				
6. Are actors and professional athletes paid too much?				

When you are finished all of your arguments, discuss and review each fallacy that was used with your partner. If your partner didn't hear the fallacy you used, start that discussion again and work through it together until he or she is able to identify the fallacy you used.

Additional Vocabulary

Word	Part of Speech	Definition	Sample Sentence

Appendix

Note the following regarding these notes:

- the use of abbreviations and short forms
- how some things are underlined to form a heading
- the use of arrows and bullet points to organize things
- the empty space on the right side of the page (good for adding material later)
- the use of indentations and a shifting margin (this makes things easier to see)
- the use of a question mark (?) when something is missed (get it from a classmate later)

Compare these notes with your own.

The Music of Lang. & the Lang. of Mus.

What do we all share as humans?
" abilities define us?

Amazon Tribe
⌐ - no possessions, #s or counting
  - no visual art, no terms for colour
  - no creation myth
  + have lang. & music (songs)
       ⌐ L.   ⌐ M.

Every culture has L. & M. (human universal)

What's in common w̄ M. & L.?
⌐ + rhythm (pattern)
  + melody (" of ???)
  + syntax
  + affect (???)

But how similar in detail?
⌐ - rhythm has beat / L. doesn't
  - melody uses pitch / "
  - syntax is present / Instrumental M. doesn't
  - Emotions in M. & L. similar → but more complex?

Tension exists btwn similarities & diff. of M. & L.

Focus on Instr. M.

What's New? → Empirical work

2 hidden connections:
   1. Rhythm } & how they're related
   2. Syntax

Start w̄ 1.
      ⌐

Suggested answers for Skills Focus: Reading an Exam Question exercise (Chapter 4, pages 69–70)

Directive	Your Notes
classify	Into what general category(ies) does this idea belong? Divide cat(s) accordingly.
compare	What are the similarities among these ideas?
contrast	What are the differences between these ideas?
critique	What are the strengths and weaknesses of this idea?
define	What does this word or phrase mean?
demonstrate	What proof or evidence can I find to clearly defend this idea?
describe	What are the important characteristics or features of this idea?
discuss	What are the important factors of this issue, and how are they related to each other or a central idea?
evaluate	What are the arguments for and against this idea? Which arguments are stronger?
explain	Why is this the case?
identify	What is this idea? What is its name?
interpret	What does this idea mean? Why is it important?
justify	Why is this correct? Why is this true?
outline	What are the main points and essential details?
summarize	Briefly, what are the important ideas?
trace	What is the sequence of ideas or order of events?

Proofreading Sample

This is an authentic example of a university student's essay on the novel *The Pearl*, by John Steinbeck. Note the list of items on the right that this student has proofread for. Notice also how the page is marked. Use this as a model for your own proofreading.

1

Professor Fogal

Kansai Gaidai University

9 July

What the Pearl Song Tells Readers

handwritten notes at top right:
S-V
fragm — the/an/a
Format
Capital
adj
Countable

The story begins with the beautiful image of the sky – a part of nature – as though it promised the satisfied, peaceful life of the protagonist, Kino. In Steinbeck's novel, *The Pearl*, nature that surrounds Kino is described so precisely that readers can imagine the beautiful scenery of the world. Nature, in addition to human beings, is also one of the main characters in this novel. Yet, as the title indicates, it is the pearl Kino finds in the sea that plays the most significant role of all nature. Despite the beautiful images of nature, the pearl presents an uneasy theme of the story: person versus nature.

Depictions of the music of the pearl in the novel are both positive and negative as if to show that nature has both beneficial and threatening aspects; moreover, these depictions indicates the inevitable defeat of a person when a person challenges nature.

The Pearl presents readers three types of music in it: the music of the family, the music of evil (also referred as the music of the enemy), and the music of the pearl. These three kinds of music are closely related to Kino's feeling. At many points in the story, Kino hears music. Two of them – the music of the family and evil give quite opposite impressions for readers. The music of the family – Kino hears it when he feels peaceful and happy – gives readers positive impressions. Descriptions of the music of the family show pleasantness. In contrast, the music of evil – as it literally means, can

Photo Credits

1 iStockphoto.com/JackJelly; **2** (bl) TM & Copyright 1947 Catechetical Guild, (bc) Swiss Movement/John Collins © McCord Museum, (br) "CCCP–USA Superman" by Roman Cieslewicz, 1968, © Estate of Roman Cieslewicz/SODRAC (2011); **20** © EXPA/David Rawcliffe/NewSport/Corbis; **21** (l) AudioFuel, (r) Art by Joe Fafa/Photo by Jose A. Blazquez Rico; **23** Bloomberg/Getty Images; **39** iStockphoto.com/Alain Couillaud; **40** (l) iStockphoto.com/Justin Long, (r) NASA; **42** © Roger LeLievre; **58** Fred Hoare/Belfast Telegraph; **59** (tl, tr, bl) © Robert White, (cl, cr, br) Fred Hoare/Belfast Telegraph; **73** UN Photo/H Vassal; **79** Maxx Images/Shahidul Alam; **92** Veer/Matthew Browning; **100** (t) Ben Hider/Getty Images Entertainment/Getty Images, (b) Stephen Lovekin/Getty Images Entertainment/Getty Images; **102** Mike Powell/Getty Images Sport/Getty Images; **110** iStockphoto.com/Anne Clark; **111** (tr) iStockphoto.com/Gary Radler, (c) © Institute for Aboriginal Development 1992. Developed by Lorna Wilson; **123** (cr) Reconstruction by Richard Neave, Manchester University/Photo by Antonio Scorza/Getty Images, (b) recreated with permission of George Weber; **130** bigstock/lovleah; **134** iStockphoto.com/David Marchal; **149** NASA; **150** NASA/JPL/Cornell University; **152** NASA Headquarters Greatest Images of NASA; **158** NASA (Scan by Hamish Lindsay and Colin Mackellar); **164** MILpictures by Tom Weber/Getty Images; **165** (tr) iStockphoto.com/Anthony Rosenberg, (cl) iStockphoto.com/Keith Binns, (cr) Latuff 2006; **167** Michael Leunig; **168** Peter Power/GetStock.com; **172** iStockphoto.com/Wouter van Caspel

Literary Credits

3–4 Adapted from "Causes of the Cold War" by Shmoop University, Inc. (www.shmoop.com)

10–11 Lyrics © 1963 by Warner Bros Inc.; renewed 1991 by Special Rider Music

14–15 Summarizing Key Points inspired by "Expressions for text analysis" worksheet at http://www.eslhandouts.com/worksheets/expression-for-text-analysis-presentation/

22–24 With the exception of the first and last paragraph, reading adapted from "Music and Sport" on Peak Performance, http://www.pponline.co.uk/encyc/0230.htm

29 "You'll Never Walk Alone" by Richard Rodgers & Oscar Hammerstein II. Copyright © 1945 by Richard Rodgers and Oscar Hammerstein II. Copyright Renewed. International Copyright Secured. All Rights Reserved. Used by Permission of Williamson Music, A Division of Rodgers & Hammerstein: An Imagem Company.

30–32 Thinking on Your Feet adapted from: http://www.mindtools.com/pages/article/ThinkingonYourFeet.htm . © Mind Tools Ltd, 1996-2011. All rights reserved. Reproduced by permission.

37 Examples of thesis statement error types from http://www.uni-giessen.de/˜ga1070/thesis_statements.html

42–44 Paragraphs 2–17 of "Tragedies at Sea at a Glance" adapted from "The fateful voyage of the Edmund Fitzgerald" by Jenny Nolan. Published in The Detroit News, September 21, 2000 http://apps.detnews.com/apps/history/index.php?id=114#ixzz1aU6expKH

51–52 Evaluating Sources of Information was inspired by material found on the website of the Purdue Online Writing Lab, http://owl.english.purdue.edu/owl/resource/553/04/

55–56 A number of suggested expressions used for presentations were found in "Presenting a Seminar Paper: Useful Language" http://www.uefap.com/speaking/spkfram.htm

69-70 and 184 Table adapted from material found on Indiana University's Writing Tutorial Services website http://www.indiana.edu/˜wts/pamphlets/essay_exam.shtml

77–78 Apartheid at a Glance paragraphs 1–8 adapted with permission from Thomas Hazlett, "Apartheid," in David R. Henderson, ed., The Concise Encyclopedia of Economics, Indianapolis: Liberty Fund, 2008.

78–79 Apartheid at a Glance paragraphs 9–1 2 adapted from "Anti-Apartheid movement in South Africa proved triumphant" by Dan Heymann. http://www.weeping.info/anti-apartheid-movement.html

83–84 "WEEPING"
Written by Dan Heymann
Published by Muffled Music
Administered by Kobalt Music Publishing
Also administered by Geoff Paynter Music Publishing

94–95 Race Relations in America at a Glance Excerpts from pages 1-5 of Black Noise: Rap Music and Black Culture in Contemporary America (Wesleyan University Press 1994) © 1994 by Tricia Rose and reprinted by permission of Wesleyan University Press.

100 KRS-One quotation from http://blogcritics.org/music/article/q-rap-vs-hip-hop-whats/

100–1 About the Artists adapted from http://www.rollingstone.com/music/artists/public-enemy

101–2 Fear of a Black Planet.
Words and Music by Eric Sadler, Keith Boxley, Carleton Ridenhour, Leroy Bonner, Marshall Jones, Ralph Middlebrooks, Walter Morrison, Norman Napier, Andrew Noland, Marvin Pierce and Gregory Webster Copyright © 1990 DEF AMERICAN SONGS, INC., BRING THE NOIZE, INC. and BRIDGEPORT MUSIC, INC.
All Rights for DEF AMERICAN SONGS, INC. Controlled and Administered by SONGS OF UNIVERSAL, INC.
All Rights Reserved Used by Permission
Reprinted by Permission of Hal Leonard Corporation

"Fear of a Black Planet"
written by Chuck D, Eric Sadler, Keith Boxlee, Leroy Bonner, Marshall Jones, Ralph Middlebrooks, Walter Morrison, and Norman Napier
(c) 1990 Reach Music Publishing, Inc., Terrordome Music Publishing, LLC (BMI), Your Mother's Music. Inc. Used by permission. All rights reserved.

105–6 Example about the Senator adapted from http://www.criticalreading.com/inference_reading.htm

107–8 The Writing Center, University of North Carolina at Chapel Hill, http://writingcenter.unc.edu/resources/handouts-demos/citation/editing-and-proofreading

112 Timeline adapted by permission of Multicultural SA, Attorney-General's Department, South Australia

113–4 Paragraphs 1–6 inspired by text from http://www.pilotguides.com/destination_guide/pacific/australia/history_of_aborigines.php

114–5 Paragraphs 7–12: Text adapted courtesy of ReconciliACTION, www.reconciliACTION.org.au

115 Excerpt of Prime Minister Kevin Rudd's was reproduced from the Parliament of Australia website with the kind permission of the Commonwealth of Australia (Department of Parliamentary Services). The item can be downloaded for free from http://australia.gov.au/about-australia/our-country/our-people/apology-to-australias-indigenous-peoples subject to copyright conditions.

120–1 Took the Children Away
Words and Music by Archibald Roach
Copyright © 1990 by Mushroom Music Pty. Ltd. (APRA)
All Rights in the United States and Canada Administered by Chrysalis Music (ASCAP)
International Copyright Secured All Rights Reserved
Reprinted by Permission of Hal Leonard Corporation

122 "You can't escape the lecture..." Adapted excerpt from "How To Take Lecture Notes" by Gene Grzywacz. http://ezinearticles.com/?How-To-Take-Lecture-Notes&id=654857

124–5 "Unity and Coherence" adapted from material at http://www.writingcentre.ubc.ca/workshop/tools/unity.htm . Used courtesy of the UBC Writing Centre.

131 Discovery of DNA quotation from LI News Tonight, April 21, 2009.

132 All news headings retrieved from http://archives.cbc.ca.

139 "Wheat Kings" (Johnny Fay/Gord Downie/Robert Baker/Gordon Sinclair/Paul Langlois). Copyright © 1993 by Southern Music Publishing Co Canada/Little Smoke Music Copyright © Renewed. International Rights Secured. Used by Permission. All Rights Reserved.

140–2: "Hurricane Carter Case is Back in Court" Adapted from The New York Times, March 30, 1987 © 1987 The New York Times. All rights reserved. Used by permission and protected by the Copyright Laws of the United States. The printing, copying, redistribution, or retransmission of this Content without express written permission is prohibited.

151–2 "Space Exploration at a Glance" Adapted from "Apollo 11 Mission: Kennedy's Dream" (c) 2011 Nick Greene (http://space.about.com). Used with permission of About Inc., which can be found online at www.about.com. All rights reserved.

156–7 "Saturn 5" Written by Clint Boon, Martyn Walsh, Graham Lambert, Craig Gill and Tom Hingley. Published by Mute Song.

160–1 "Vocal Minority Insists It Was All Smoke and Mirrors" Adapted from The New York Times, July 14, 2009 © 2009 The New York Times. All rights reserved. Used by permission and protected by the Copyright Laws of the United States. The printing, copying, redistribution, or retransmission of this Content without express written permission is prohibited.

166 All quotations found at http://thinkexist.com/quotations/war/2.html

167 Paragraph 1 retrieved from the Stanford Encyclopedia of Philosophy http://plato.stanford.edu/entries/war/

167–8 Paragraphs 3-8 of "Elements of War at a Glance" adapted from "Just War Theory" and "The Philosophy of War" by Alexander Moseley, Internet Encyclopedia of Philosophy, http://www.iep.utm.edu/ , August 9, 2011.

168–9 "A Soldier's Perspective" adapted from "A Soldier's Life" by Russell Storring. Retrieved from http://www.cbc.ca/news/viewpoint/vp_storring/20030724.html. Courtesy of the CBC and Russell Storring.

172 David Fricke quotation from http://www.rollingstone.com/music/blogs/alternate-take/frickes-picks-indie-rock-history-lessons-20080717

173–4 "Intervention" Written by Arcade Fire. Permission to publish granted by Quest Management.

175–6 "Writing the In-Class Essay Exam" By Emily Schiller. http://www.back2college.com/inclassessay.htm

177–8 Discussion of the SQ3R Study Method based on Francis Pleasant Robinson, Effective Study (1970). New York: Harper & Row.

178 Table adapted from material found on www.teach-nology.com

For more information on the artists discussed in this book, please visit their websites.
Bob Dylan: www.bobdylan.com
Gerry and the Pacemakers: www.gerryandthepacemakers.co.uk
Gordon Lightfoot: www.lightfoot.ca
U2: www.u2.com
Vusi Mahlasela: vusimahlasela.com
Public Enemy: www.publicenemy.com
Archie Roach: www.archieroach.com.au
The Tragically Hip: www.thehip.com
Inspiral Carpets: www.inspiralcarpets.com
Arcade Fire: www.arcadefire.com